The Triune GOD

110 Bridge Street, Box 327
Wheaton, Illinois 60189-0327

Revised Edition
10   9
9   8   7   6   5   4   3

ISBN 0-910566-09-7

CONTENTS

THE NATURE
OF GOD

The study of God is the greatest one in which man can engage. It is one subject which is truly inexhaustible. The source for all knowledge of God is God Himself who has chosen to reveal Himself to men through the universe which He created and the Scriptures which He inspired. Theologians speak of *natural theology* (that which can be known of God through nature) and *revealed theology* (that which can be known of God through the Scriptures).

There are certain evidences of God which rise from man's observation of the world about him. To those who have eyes to see, "the heavens declare the glory of God; and the firmament showeth his handiwork" (Ps. 19:1). God is the great need of the vast creation in which we live, and consequently He must exist. One might as well think of throwing a rope into the air and climbing up, or building a tower on nothing and expecting it to stand, as to explain creation without a creator.

Is a knowledge of nature or natural theology sufficient for a knowledge of God? Read Romans 1:18-25. Here is a picture of the heathen to whom God speaks through nature. The statement of Paul that "the world by wisdom knew not God" (I Cor. 1:21) is strictly true of the history of religious systems. No heathen religion ever embodied the true conception of God, though some have had most monstrous ideas of Him. Man needs the revelation of God's Word and God's Son to really know God.

GOD IS A LIVING BEING
Shown by Nature
There is much evidence in nature to substantiate faith in the existence of God. Using facts found in nature, Christian theologians over the centuries have developed rational arguments to attest God's existence. The most enduring of these are:

Cosmological Argument
For every effect there must be a corresponding cause. Since the universe (cosmos) is an effect there must be a cause adequate to bring it into existence. That cause is God.

Teleological Argument
The Greek word for "bring to an end, finish, complete, carry out" is *teleo*. Our world reveals intelligence, harmony, and purpose. From the evidences of design and purpose in the universe as studied through the telescope and the microscope, it must be concluded that the cause or creator is intelligent.

5

Moral Argument

Since man is a moral being, possessing a sense of right and wrong, his creator and judge must be moral.

Ontological Argument

Since the concept of the absolute being is necessary in man's thinking, such an absolute being must in point of fact exist. If this is not the case, then all of man's reasonings are merely relative. The Greek word *ontos* means "in point of fact" or "in reality" or "truly."

Religious Argument

Archaeologists and anthropologists tell us that mankind throughout history has been religious. No culture has been or now is totally devoid of religion. Since the phenomenon of religion is universal there must be some truth to it.

Perhaps none of these arguments alone carries compelling proof but together they testify forcibly to the reasonableness of Christian belief in a living God.

Affirmed by Scripture

Scripture gives unqualified affirmation to the existence of God. The opening phrase of Genesis, "In the beginning God," sets forth the basic assumption of the Bible which in the rest of the Scriptures is never denied or even debated. So indelibly impressed on virtually every page of the Word is the Living God that to consent to its teachings is to brand atheism as sheer heresy. The best that the Bible can say of the atheist is that he is a fool whose reasonings stem from the heart rather than the mind (Ps. 14:1; 53:1).

GOD IS A PERSONAL BEING

The fact that God is a person is of great consequence. It is because God is a person that revelation, fellowship, and prayer are not only possible, but also meaningful. God is not mere energy or blind force, nor is He the sum total of everything (pantheism). Rather God is a person who speaks, hears, sends, and blesses among other activities. Because God is a person, man can trust Him, know Him, love Him, worship Him, and serve Him. The fact that God is a person is clearly revealed in the Scriptures.

The Multitude of Biblical Inferences

Throughout the Bible names and personal pronouns are ascribed to God which undeniably prove that He is a person. In addition to this, He is everywhere pictured as possessing the three essentials of personality — intellect, emotion, will. The Bible clearly asserts that God knows (Ps. 139:1-6), God feels (Nahum 1:2, 3; John 3:16), and God wills (I Thess. 4:3; 5:18).

The Explicit Biblical Statement (Exod. 3:13,14)

Moses had been commissioned to declare to enslaved Israel that the God of their fathers had sent him to deliver them from bondage.

Moses said, "Behold . . . they shall say to me, What is his name? what shall I say unto them?" God's answer was, "I AM THAT I AM. . . . Thus shalt thou say unto the children of Israel, I AM hath sent me unto you."

This name is most significant. The main idea is that of self-existence and personality. The words signify the eternal God, "which art, and wast, and art to come" (Rev. 11:17). This likely is the origin of the Hebrew personal name for God, *Jehovah*. This name occurs in the Old Testament over 6,000 times. Each occurence is a testimony to the personality of God.

GOD IS A SPIRIT BEING
The Teaching of Christ (Luke 24:39; John 4:24)
Grammatically simple but theologically profound is the statement, "God is spirit," uttered by the Lord in response to the Samaritan woman's query. This remarkable statement deals directly with the nature of God as is clearly seen when "a," the indefinite article which is never found in the Greek, is deleted. In His very essence God is spirit.

The basic meaning of spirit is clarified by the Lord's remark to His followers after the resurrection. When they saw Him they were terrified thinking Him to be a spirit. He banished those fears by stating that "a spirit hath not flesh and bones as ye see me have." From this it is apparent that spirit stands in contrast to that which is material or corporeal. God, being spirit, is not composed of material parts. For this reason it is true that "no man hath seen God at any time" (John 1:18).

The Second Commandment (Exod. 20:4, 5; Ps. 145:3)
The Ten Commandments are best understood in the light of the nature of God. The second commandment illustrates this principle. Because God is spirit He cannot faithfully be represented by anything which is material. Any tangible visible object, no matter how cleverly fashioned, serves only to distort the worshiper's comprehension of God. Not only is the concept distorted by the image but also it is limited. That which is material is limited to time and space whereas God being spirit is limited by neither.

The Image of God (II Cor. 4:4; Col. 1:15)
If God were of a material or bodily nature, He could be reproduced, but God is not of the nature of the material world since He cannot be seen with material eyes (John 1:18). In fact, Moses was told that no man could look upon God's face and live (Ex. 33:20). If God is spirit, what is meant by the statement that man was made in the image of God (Gen. 1:27)? Elsewhere the Bible declares that this image consists in righteousness, knowledge, holiness (Col.

3:10; Eph. 4:24). The image of God in man, therefore, consists in personal and moral likeness rather than in physical resemblance.

GOD IS ONE BEING

Christianity vs. Polytheism (Deut. 6:4, 5; I Kings 8:60; Isa. 42:8, 9; 44:6-8; 45:5, 6, 12; 46:9; Mark 12:29, 30; John 10:30; I Cor. 8:4; Eph. 4:6; I Tim. 2:5)

There was abundant reason that the first commandment should have been thundered from Sinai's summit. The worship of the sun, as the most prominent and most powerful agent in the kingdom of nature, was widely disseminated through the nations of the ancient world. In Egypt the sun was worshiped under the title Ra. Baal of the Phoenicians, Molech of the Ammonites, Hadad of the Syrians, and Bel of the Babylonians, were also deities of the sun. The worship of the sun and moon and other heavenly bodies is one of the sins most unsparingly denounced in Scripture. One of the first warnings to Israel was to take heed "lest thou lift up thine eyes unto heaven, and when thou seest the sun, and the moon, and the stars, even all the host of heaven, should be driven to worship them, and serve them" (Deut. 4:19). The utter overthrow of the nation was predicted should this law be violated, and as for the nation, so for the individual. Any man, woman, or child who worshiped the sun, or moon, or any of the hosts of heaven, when convicted of working "such abomination," was to be put to death (Deut. 17:2-5).

Israel lived in the midst of polytheistic nations (Josh. 24:2, 14, 15; Judges 10:6; II Kings 17:33). It appears that the great purpose in their being called out as a chosen and separate people was to witness to the unity of God. No other truth receives more prominence in the Old Testament. More than fifty passages teach that God is one, that there is no other, and that He has no equal.

It is to be expected, then, if the Lord is one God, that the first and great commandment is the unity of all man's powers in concert and concentration on loving God (Deut. 6:4, 5; Mark 12:29, 30). An undivided God justly claims the undivided allegiance and worship of His creatures. He will not recognize any other claimant to divine honor: "My glory will I not give to another, neither my praise to graven images" (Isa. 42:8). All human religion is an abomination to God, and it is not for us to try to discover how much good there is in beliefs that fail to give God His undisputed right to exclusive worship. God will not accept a niche in the pantheon of heathendom. He must be all or nothing.

Christianity vs. Unitarianism (Gen. 1:26; 3:22; Isa. 6:8; Matt. 3:16, 17; II Cor. 13:14)

From the earliest centuries of the church, evangelical Christians have insisted upon the doctrine of the Trinity. This doctrine has been defined by A. H. Strong, "In the nature of God there are three eternal distinctions and these three are equal: not merely three persons in one, or three Gods in one, nor that God manifests Himself in three ways. There are three essential distinctions in the subsistence of God." The Trinitarian doctrine has been assailed vigorously by various types of Unitarians through the centuries. Unitarianism charges that Trinitarianism is nothing more than tritheism or veiled sophisticated polytheism thus violating the oneness of God.

While the term *trinity* is not a biblical expression, the doctrine of the Trinity is biblical. It is totally a product of revelation which man's reason could never discover. The doctrine is to be believed because the inspired Scriptures teach it. It is one of the most profound and difficult mysteries in the Word of God. Although the truth of the Trinity lies outside the capacity of our minds to fully comprehend and explain, the doctrine is clearly taught in the Bible. God is unique in this respect. There is nothing in nature which perfectly illustrates this aspect of God's being. Examples such as a circle divided into three parts; light, heat, energy; three musical notes comprising a chord; ice, water, steam; body, soul, and spirit of man all fall short of clarifying the truth which they seek to illustrate.

Although the Old Testament is not as explicit as the New Testament in this area of truth, there are strong inferences which are best explained in the light of the Trinity. The plural pronouns *us* and *our* (Gen. 1:26; 11:7; Isa. 6:8) cannot speak of creatures such as men and angels hence must speak of God. Passages referring to the Messiah (Isa. 9:6; Micah 5:2; Ps. 45:6, 7) indicate that He is one with Jehovah and yet distinct from Him. The Angel of Jehovah is described in similar manner (Gen. 16:9, 13; 22:11, 16; 31:11-13; 48:15, 16; Ex. 4:2, 4, 5; Judg. 13:20-22). The Hebrew word for God, *Elohim,* is actually a plural form although generally it takes a singular verb. These and other inferences in the Old Testament may find an explanation in the doctrine of the Trinity.

It is in the New Testament that the truth becomes more precise. Clearly the New Testament teaches the complete deity of the Father, Son, and Holy Spirit while at the same time distinguishing between them. Only the doctrine of the Trinity does justice to the plain teachings of the New Testament.

That the doctrine of the Trinity is taught in Scripture, there can be no doubt. By comparing Scripture with Scripture, it can be known even if it cannot be perfectly understood. In subsequent lessons we shall see how frequently and plainly the Bible teaches not only that Jesus Christ and the Holy Spirit possess the same essence as God the Father, but that they are equal with Him in power and glory. One illustration will suffice at this time:

The Father is God — Romans 1:7.
The Son is God — Hebrews 1:8.
The Holy Spirit is God — Acts 5:3, 4.
The New Testament clearly recognizes each member of the Trinity as true Deity and presents its message upon this premise.

REVIEW QUESTIONS

1. In what two ways can knowledge of God be secured?
2. What is our most complete source for knowledge of God?
3. What are the rational arguments for the existence of God?
4. What is the basic assumption of the Scriptures?
5. Give biblical evidence to prove that God is a person.
6. Of what practical significance is the fact that God is a person?
7. What is meant by "spirit"?
8. How does the second commandment indicate that God is a spirit?
9. What is meant by the statement that man was made in the image of God?
10. How did the call of Israel witness to the unity of God?
11. Briefly state the doctrine of the Trinity in your own words.
12. Why is the doctrine of the Trinity to be believed?

APPLYING DOCTRINE TO LIFE

1. Why is it imperative that church leaders and teachers know about the nature of God?
2. How should a knowledge of God affect a teacher's ministry?

THE INFINITUDE OF GOD

2

The psalmist wrote "Great is the Lord, and greatly to be praised; and his greatness is unsearchable" (Ps. 145:3). Even the atomic age with its vast scientific knowledge does not change this humble confession. The Bible clearly sets forth the attributes of God but each characteristic has a dimension which is beyond human comprehension. All that God is He is to the perfect or infinite degree. Man being finite in his being and understanding cannot measure God. He only can stand in awe of His greatness. To acknowledge this unsearchable, limitless dimension we speak of the infinitude of God.

GOD IS ETERNAL

To confess that God is eternal is to affirm that His life is infinite.

We cannot fathom the unknown future, but we might think back as far as the mind can go and try to imagine eternity. We speak of Genesis as the book of the beginnings. We read of the beginning of the nations, the beginning of man, the beginning of creation. But that was not the beginning. We may go back to the time when the angels were created — those sublime, empyreal (or celestial) Sons of God, who were present to sing an oratorio on that prehistoric day when the earth was created (Job 38:7). But that was not the beginning. We may enter eternity where God the Creator dwelt alone, with all creation resting in His mighty, gigantic thought. We may go back, back, back as far as our imagination can fly, and yet never arrive at the beginning, for there is no beginning or end to eternity.

While God has created such immortal beings as angels and men, He alone is without beginning, and thus may be said to be the sole inhabitant of eternity. Men have a past, present, and future; God knows only the present, for both past and future are "now" to Him. Men are everlasting; God is eternal (Deut. 32:40; Ps. 90:2; I Tim. 6:16).

Alpha and omega are the first and last letters of the Greek alphabet, the language in which the New Testament was originally written. The use of these letters in Revelation 1:8 indicates that God was at the very beginning and will be at the end of all time. While eternity has neither beginning nor end, time has both. Time is swallowed up in eternity, and none can comprehend eternity but the eternal God.

GOD IS IMMUTABLE

God only is unchanging and unchangeable. God is above all

causes of change and even the possibility of it. This unchangeableness or immutability of God is closely associated with His immensity (He exceeds space to the infinite degree) and eternity (He exceeds time to the infinite degree). In contrast to the ever changing world, of Him it can be said, "They shall be changed: But thou art the same" (Ps. 102:26, 27).

God Cannot Change His Nature

As an infinite and absolute being, self-existent and absolutely independent, God is exalted above all the causes and even the possibilities of a change. He can neither increase nor decrease. He is subject to no process of development or self-evolution. His knowledge and power can never be greater or less. He can neither be wiser nor holier; He cannot be more righteous nor more merciful than He ever has been or ever will be. He is absolutely above all law that governs time and change, for His word is law.

God cannot change in His relation to men. What encouragement would there be to lift up our eyes to one who was of one mind this day and another mind tomorrow? Would we trust a vacillating ruler? It was because God is unchangeable in His mercy that there was hope for apostate Israel: "I am the Lord, I change not; therefore ye sons of Jacob are not consumed" (Mal. 3:6).

God Cannot Change His Word (Ps. 119:160; Matt. 5:18; John 10:35b)

It is the most natural thing in the world for man's word to be broken. Why is it that our friends and relatives have a legal, written form for the slightest business transactions? Isn't it because we may fully expect man's spoken word to be broken? Is not man a changeable creature? How many times have we been deceived by those in whom we placed confidence? Is not man a limited creature? Does he not often find himself a victim of circumstances and unable to fulfill his obligations, however much he may desire to do so? Altogether, then, it is not only possible but quite probable that man's word will be broken. In sharp contrast we find that the word of God remains the same.

God Cannot Change His Will (I Sam. 15:11; Jer. 26:13)

If God cannot change, how do we explain the Bible passages which speak of God as "repenting"?

This repentant attitude of God does not involve any real change in His character and purpose. He ever hates sin, and ever pities and loves the sinner. This attitude is just as true before as after the sinner's repentance. There is no change fundamentally in God's attitude, although He may change his *dealings* in view of man's change. For example, God's attitude toward the wickedness of Israel did not change. He hated her sin, and because she persisted in associating herself with sin, of necessity she shared its penalties.

But when Israel, whom God always loved and pitied, repented and separated herself from her sin, God's dealing with her in consequence changed. As Strong says, "God's immutability is not that of the stone, that has no internal experience, but rather that of the column of mercury, that rises and falls with every change in the temperature of the surrounding atmosphere. God may will a change, but He cannot change His will."

GOD IS OMNISCIENT

By omniscience is meant that God's knowledge is infinite. The knowledge of God is as precise, minute, and certain as it is vast and all-embracing. All that He says and does is absolutely true and right. He is too wise to make any mistakes. He can neither err nor fail. We have but to dwell upon this vast subject to cry out like Paul in wonder and astonishment, "O the depth of the riches both of the wisdom and knowledge of God" (Rom. 11:33).

God Knows All the Past (Acts 15:18; I John 3:20)

Man is a forgetful creature. Even with the benefit of papers and books with which to refresh his memory, he remembers little of the past. True, he may study what has been recorded on the pages of history. He may dig down and unearth the archives of ancient nations to learn something about the past. But how imperfect his knowledge and how quickly he forgets it!

God Knows All the Present

God's Perfect Knowledge of Nature (Gen. 15:5; Ps. 147:4, 5; Isa. 40:26)

God challenged Abraham to count the stars that he might have some conception of the great numbers that would constitute his descendants. But no scientist of Abraham's day would have ventured to compare the stars with the sands of the sea (Gen. 22:17). Hipparchus, the ancient astronomer, counted 1,022, and later Ptolemy recorded 1,026. Jeremiah's declaration that the host of heaven could not be numbered (Jer. 33:22) would seem a scientific inaccuracy were it not for the fact that our latest instruments have revealed an almost inconceivable and incalculable number of stars.

But while man even today cannot count the stars, God not only knows the number but the names of every one. Can you conceive of any man having sufficient knowledge to call every one of the millions of inhabitants of this globe by name? And yet God knows the names of all the stars in our own galaxy, and an incalculable number in ten million other galaxies.

God's Perfect Knowledge of Men

    (1) Man's ways (Ps. 119:168; 139:3; Job 24:23; Prov. 5:21; Heb. 4:13)

    (2) Man's words (Ps. 19:14; 139:4)

(3) Man's thoughts (Ps. 139:2; Luke 11:17; I Cor. 3:20)

(4) Man's desires (Acts 1:24; Rom. 8:27)

God Knows All the Future (Isa. 41:21-23; 42:9; 46:10; 48:5-7)

In no way is the Bible better attested as the Word of God than in its revelation of God's foreknowledge. More than one-fourth of the Bible is prophecy. We have but to read what God said would be the end of Babylon and Nineveh, and then walk through the ruins of these once magnificent cities, to realize God's foreknowledge.

No prophet gives us a greater glimpse of God's foreknowledge than Isaiah. Judah was to be carried away by the powerful armies of Babylon. All the prophets had declared that, but it was left for Isaiah to challenge the gods of Babylon, if they were gods at all, to declare things to come.

Very minutely Isaiah foretells the coming of Cyrus, the conqueror of Babylon (45:1-4; 46:11). This prophecy was spoken when Assyria, and not Babylon, was in the ascendancy, and it was spoken of Persia, an inferior nation. In fact, the name of Cyrus was thus revealed 180 years before he was born.

Christ again and again predicted His crucifixion and resurrection (Matt. 16:21; 17:22, 23; 20:17-19; 26:1, 2). He thus proved not only that He knew the future, but that He was God. These predictions were so seemingly improbable and even impossible that the disciples were not able to comprehend them (Mark 8:31-33; 9:31, 32; 10:33).

There is not a thing which shall transpire in the next thousand years which is not already known to the infinite mind of God. There is not a deed which shall be transacted tomorrow or the next day, or the next; there is nothing that shall transpire in eternity, but God knows it altogether.

God's Right Use of Knowledge (Isa. 40:13, 14)

With all man's knowledge he lacks the necessary wisdom to make a right use of that knowledge. Man is constantly making mistakes. "To err is human." But not so with God; His wisdom is infinite. Only God is removed beyond the possibility of making a mistake. He never experiments; He never changes His plans. The ages have not taught Him anything, and He cannot improve upon what He has already done, for His wisdom assures perfection in the first place.

God's Wisdom in Creation (Prov. 3:19; Isa. 40:12)

In a musical instrument there is first the skill of the workman in the construction, then of the artisan in tuning its strings, and finally the technique of the musician in expressing the beauty of its tones. So in the works of creation we see the wisdom of God, first in framing the world, then in tuning its parts into perfect harmony, and finally, in expressing its marvelous utility in His wise government of all its creatures. The wisdom of creation appears in:

Its Variety (Ps. 104:24; I Cor. 15:41)

One never completes his studies of zoology or botany, for there appear to be endless species of creatures and a countless variety of plants. There are wonderful similarities, and yet even more marvelous differences in two leaves growing on the same tree. Even "one star differeth from another star in glory."

Its Beauty and Harmony (Eccles. 3:11)

The lilies of the field are more beautiful and fragrant than the most exquisite artificial flower. The movements of the planets in perfect harmony with each other are what constitute the safety and sublimity of the solar system.

Its Fitness and Usefulness (Prov. 30:24-28)

Divine wisdom is more marvelous in its purposes than in its creation. There is a spider on the wall, but he takes hold on king's palaces and spins his web to rid the world of noxious flies. There is a tiny sea creature under the water, but it builds an island. The star in the sky guides a great vessel.

God's Wisdom in Providence (Ps. 104:13, 14, 27, 28)

This can be shown in a multitude of ways. One example is the earth. We know how thin a covering of the surface of the earth is the atmosphere, that envelope of gases surrounding the earth, which sustains life. The atmosphere, so little appreciated because of its seeming abundance, is the medium of both light and sound and the means of both heat and protection.

The Medium of Light

If it were not for the air about us, it would be dark except where the sun shines directly upon us. At sunrise, we would be plunged into immediate daylight, and at sunset, into immediate darkness. It would not get lighter or darker gradually; there would be no dawn or twilight.

The Medium of Sound

If it were not for the air, we could never make or hear a sound of any kind. All sounds are made and carried by air vibrations.

The Means of Heat

The atmosphere serves as a blanket to hold the heat of the sun. Except for this air-blanket around the earth, the daytime heat would be too great and the cold at night would be too severe for life to exist on the earth. It is the atmosphere which makes artificial heat possible.

The Means of Protection

Were there no atmosphere, thousands of meteorites, traveling in space and attracted to the earth, would fall with deadly impact upon its surface. The atmosphere serves as a cushion to arrest their velocity and break the violence of their fall.

God's Wisdom in Redemption

Christ, the Wisdom of God (I Cor. 1:24)

Wise Men went to Jerusalem to find the King of Kings, but the poor humble shepherds went to Bethlehem and found Christ at once. God chose a lowly manger instead of a king's splendid palace as the birthplace of His Son. None was poorer, none humbler, none more lowly from an earthly standpoint than the only Redeemer of God's elect. Therefore, no one can say Christianity is only for the wise, the wealthy, or the noble. God makes it possible for *all* sinners to be saved, and makes their salvation depend not upon their wisdom, but upon their faith.

The Church, the Wisdom of God (I Cor. 1:21)

God chose twelve uneducated men to evangelize the world, to make it evident that it is the wisdom of the gospel and not the wisdom of men that wins human hearts. God chose not warriors but weaklings to proclaim the gospel, and the "foolishness" of their message conquered continents. They spread the gospel, and the Lord received the glory — not the apostles.

GOD IS OMNIPOTENT

God's power is infinite and admits of no bounds or limitations except His own will. For Him to think, is to act; to resolve, is to execute. "Hath he said and shall he not do it?" He speaks and it is done. Since His wisdom is perfect, He does not experiment, but once for all executes a work which cannot be improved upon.

God's Power in Creation (Ps. 33:4-9; Isa. 40:12-17)

The first chapter of Genesis is not the only account of creation in the Bible. God's marvelous wisdom and power in the construction of the earth are reiterated again and again. The psalmist declared that by God's word the heavens were made, and that the starry host was brought into existence by "the breath of his mouth."

When we are inclined to feel the world is getting larger and man is growing great, it is well to read Isaiah 40. Note specifically how God's power is magnified in verses 12-17.

God's Power in Providence (Jer. 32:17-24)

Jeremiah was in prison when he offered this wonderful prayer. This was in the last days of Jerusalem when the city was being besieged by Nebuchadnezzar. Because the faithful prophet persisted in proclaiming the ultimate capture of the city, he was imprisoned. But his sad predicament did not lessen his faith in the Almighty. He approached God with an acknowledgment that there is nothing too hard for Him who made the heaven and the earth (vs. 17), and it is interesting to notice that when his prayer was finished, God answered him in the same language of His omnipotence (vs. 27). Jeremiah magnified God's power in His specific dealings with Israel (vss. 20-24).

God's Power Over Nature (Ps. 107:25-29; Matt. 8:24-27)

In Psalm 107 we have a picture of a storm at sea. The towering waves threaten to overwhelm the vessel as it rides one moment on the crest of the billow and then drops down to the depths beneath. The sailors stagger on deck like "a drunken man, and are at their wits' end." But how quickly the storm subsides and the waves are still when God is asked to intervene. God's special intervention in the laws of nature is called a miracle. These miracles in nature were not limited to the time of Christ, for many today can testify to remarkable answers to prayer, when rain has been provided, a scourge of insects has been stayed, a forest fire has been diverted.

God's Power Over Man (Exod. 5:2; 12:30, 31; Dan. 4:30-37)

Some of the world's greatest monarchs defied Almighty God only to discover that all kings owe their place and power to God (Prov. 8:15, 16). When the great Napoleon set out to conquer Russia at the head of the Grand Army of Europe, someone reminded him that "man proposes but God disposes." The conqueror of Europe replied, "I am he that both proposes and disposes." His magnificent army seemed invincible, but God used tiny snowflakes to overwhelm it. The flower of European militia perished in the snowbanks of Russia. And God also used a storm to defeat the Invincible Armada of Philip II of Spain.

God's Power Over Satan (Job 1:10, 12; 2:6; Luke 22:31, 32)

Satan, a fallen angel and the prince of the powers of darkness, is called the god of this world (II Cor. 4:4), so completely does he dominate it. But Satan has no power over any of God's children except as God allows. This fact is clearly established in the cases of Job and Peter. God can set a limit to the power of Satan just as He can stop the raging waves of the ocean. One day the Lord God omnipotent will reign over heaven and earth, and the devil will be "cast into the lake of fire and brimstone, where the beast and the false prophet are, and shall be tormented day and night for ever and ever" (Rev. 20:10).

God's Power in Redemption (Acts 9:3-6; 16:30-34)

How quickly God transformed the lives of Saul, the persecutor, and the jailer of Philippi who was about to commit suicide! Thousands today could give similar testimony to the saving power of God. One of the most convincing accounts of the grace of God is that of the transformation of the savage spear-ruled Auca Indians who came under the influence of the gospel through the martyrdom of the five missionaries in Ecuador. This dramatic account is told in story and picture in Elizabeth Elliot's *The Savage My Kinsman*.

God's Power to Will

God's omnipotence is dependent upon His will. Even greater than God's omnipotence is His perfect character which controls it. Character is not so much made up of impulses as restraints. God's high moral character makes it impossible for Him to misuse His omnipotence. God's will, then, is dependent upon His character.

God is infinitely wise and cannot will what is foolish.

God is infinitely just and cannot will what is unfair.

God is infinitely good and cannot will what is evil.

God is infinitely pure and cannot will what is unholy.

GOD IS OMNIPRESENT

The omnipresence of God is closely associated with His omnipotence and omniscience. "Can any hide himself in secret places that I shall not see him? Do not I fill heaven and earth? saith the Lord" (Jer. 23:24). All-seeing presupposes God being always present. Pantheists declare that God is everything, but Scripture teaches that the Creator is apart from His creation. Astronomers have been unable to measure the bounds of the universe, thus it is most difficult for men to comprehend this attribute of God. We must accept the scriptural statement of the fact. The 139th Psalm speaks of the omniscience of God (vss. 1-6) and the omnipotence of God (vss. 13-19), but dwells particularly on His omnipresence (vss. 7-12). David realized that he was never out of the sight of God any more than he was outside of the range of His knowledge and power. From these and many other Scriptures (Jer. 23:23, 24; Job 22:12-14) it is clearly taught that God is everywhere personally present and acting.

REVIEW QUESTIONS

1. What is meant by the infinitude of God?
2. How is everlasting different from eternal?
3. Name three things God cannot change.
4. How does the fact that God is immutable benefit the believer?
5. About what three periods of time does God know everything?
6. What does God know about the stars?
7. How does God's foreknowledge prove that the Bible is the Word of God?
8. How does God's wisdom eliminate the possibility of His making a mistake?
9. How is God's wisdom shown in the events associated with the coming of Christ?
10. What suggestions of God's power in creation are shown in Isaiah 40?
11. Illustrate ways in which God's will is dependent upon His character?
12. What is the scriptural teaching concerning the omnipresence of God?

APPLYING DOCTRINE TO LIFE

1. What personal witness should be presented to a person who does not believe in the existence of God?
2. How should the omniscience of God affect one's teaching ministry?

THE HOLINESS, RIGHTEOUSNESS, AND JUSTICE OF GOD

3

If we were absolutely convinced that it were possible to find on earth any man without a fault, we would make arrangements to meet him. If there could be found a human being incapable of making a mistake, would we not want him for a friend? But we well know that such a person does not exist. Diogenes, a Greek cynic, won an imperishable name for himself by carrying a lighted lantern around the streets of Athens by day, looking for an honest man. He never found such a person. In fact, Diogenes himself was banished from his country for coining counterfeit money.

There may be a man — yes, many men — who have no desire or intention of committing a single wrong but, alas, there is no man of whom it can be said, "He *cannot* do wrong."

We have seen that God is incapable of making intellectual mistakes because of His omniscience. It is equally impossible for Him to make moral mistakes because of His holiness. And it is just as impossible for Him to render a wrong decision regarding the mistakes of others, because of His justice. "Shall not the Judge of all the earth do right?" asked Abraham when the destruction of Sodom had been revealed to him (Gen. 18:25). Yes, the Judge of all the earth *shall* do right, for we shall now learn His *holiness* places His character above possible reproach, while His *justice* makes His judgment absolutely infallible.

GOD'S HOLINESS

To be holy is to possess not one virtue or grace, but all. Even some of the best of men, who have become noted for some outstanding virtue, were pitifully lacking in others. Socrates was a model Greek, but was cruel to his wife and children. Plato and Aristotle were teachers of wisdom, but tolerant of the licentiousness of their fellow countrymen. Cato was proverbial for his honesty, but was cruel to his slaves. The strongest men have some weakness of character that unfits them for perfect holiness. The crown of supremacy belongs to God, not only by an arbitrary act of coronation, but by His own inherent fitness to wear it.

God's Holiness Taught by Express Statement (Josh. 24:19; I Sam. 2:2; Job 36:23; Ps. 99:9; Isa. 5:16; Ezek. 39:7; Rev. 4:8)

In the Old Testament

The holiness of God is emphasized throughout the Old Testament. God is called the Holy One of Israel about thirty times in Isaiah, and is so called also in Jeremiah and Ezekiel. In contrast to the idolatrous nations about it, the chosen nation was constantly impressed with the two great distinguishing characteristics of Israel's God.

He was *one* God.

He was a *holy* God.

After the law had failed to bring Israel to see the holiness of God, the prophets were sent especially to impress the people with this all-important fact. To the prophets, God was the absolutely Holy One; the One with eyes too pure to behold evil, the One swift to punish sin.

In the New Testament

The attributes of holiness are ascribed to each of the three persons of the Trinity.

God the Father is the Holy One (John 17:11)

God the Son is the Holy One (Acts 3:14)

God the Spirit is the Holy One (Acts 13:52)

The truth that God is holy is a fundamental truth of the Bible — of the Old Testament and the New Testament, of the Jewish religion and of the Christian faith.

God's Holiness Taught in the Ten Commandments (Exod. 19:10-13; 20:7-11)

The strict orders that were given to Israel in regard to approaching Sinai when God came down to utter with His own voice the Ten Commandments, were to impress the people with His holiness. While the first and second commandments made emphatic the *unity* of God, the third and fourth emphasized the *holiness* of God. What pertains unto God — His *name* and His *day* — must be kept holy. It is well to be reminded of these important commandments as well as those that relate to murder and theft.

God's Holiness Taught in the Ceremonial Law (Exod. 39:30; Lev. 11:44, 45; 19:2)

The theme of the book of Leviticus is "holiness," a word which occurs eighty-seven times in the twenty-seven chapters. Its keynote is, "Ye shall be holy; for I the Lord your God am holy." This and the other books of the Pentateuch set forth God's holiness.

The plan of the tabernacle also presented God's holiness. God's presence was especially manifested in a particular room known as the Holy of Holies, which no one could enter but the high priest, and he only once a year (Exod. 26:33; Lev. 16:2).

God's Holiness Taught in Personal Visions

In the visions of Himself which God granted men in the Scriptures, the characteristic that most impressed them was divine holiness.

Moses' Vision (Exod. 33:18-23)

The glory of the Lord which Moses was privileged to see, was in reality the glory of His holiness.

Isaiah's Vision (Isa. 6:1-5)

Isaiah was one of the holiest men in all Israel, but when he caught a glimpse of the glory of God, he realized and confessed his own sinfulness, as well as that of his people.

John's Vision (Rev. 4:8-11)

Every glimpse of heaven that John was permitted to see and record is a picture of the glory of God, and the recognition of His holiness by all the inhabitants of that place.

God's Holiness Taught by the Punishment of Profane Men

Nadab and Abihu (Lev. 10:1-3)

Nadab and Abihu were guilty of the sin of presumption. They debased their holy office of priesthood by offering strange fire before the Lord. Even though they were the sons of Aaron, it was necessary for these profane men to meet a sudden and miraculous death by fire from heaven.

Korah, Dathan, Abiram (Num. 16:4-12, 31-33)

Korah, Dathan, and Abiram also debased their high office of priesthood by rebelling against the authority of Moses and Aaron. Moses in his humility suggested that the Lord would decide between Korah and his company, and Moses and Aaron. We need to note especially the warning Moses gave to these rebellious sons of Levi. "Seemeth it but a small thing unto you, that the God of Israel hath separated you from the congregation of Israel, to bring you near to himself to do the service of the tabernacle of the Lord, and to stand before the congregation to minister unto them?" (Num. 16:9). God's immediate punishment followed when the earth opened her mouth and swallowed up Korah and all the men that were associated with him in the rebellion.

Uzziah (II Chron. 26:16-21)

Uzziah, the king of Judah, usurped the office of priesthood and ventured to burn incense unto the Lord, and while engaged in this forbidden act, the priests and the congregation observed the marks of leprosy upon his face, and he remained a leper until the day of his death.

God's Holiness Taught by the Provision of a Redeemer (Prov. 15:9, 26; Isa. 59:1, 2; Rom. 5:8-11)

Sin is an abomination in the light of God's perfect holiness, hence the sinner must be separated from God. The sinner and God are at opposite poles of the moral universe. How can God punish sin and yet be reconciled to the sinner? The answer is Jesus Christ, the only Redeemer of God's elect. The Cross shows how much God loves holiness. The Cross exhibits God's holiness even as it does His love.

God's love to sinners will never be appreciated until seen in the light of His blazing wrath against sin. Christ died not merely for our sins, but that He might provide us with that righteousness in which God delights.

GOD'S RIGHTEOUSNESS

Righteousness is the expression of God's holiness. Holiness has to do with God's character, but His holiness is expressed by righteousness in His relation to man. The righteousness of God may be said to be His *love of holiness*. This is shown by:

God's Hatred of Sin (Ps. 5:4; 11:5; Prov. 6:16; Hab. 1:13)

The presence and power of sin must be apparent to every one. Sin is the ultimate cause of every sickness and every sorrow (Gen. 3:17-19). Sin is the undertaker that digs every grave and officiates at every funeral. Sin is the occasion of all want and wretchedness, all pain and privation. There are some men who say there is no heaven. They wish to know nothing better than this earth. If this is heaven, it is a very strange one — this world of sickness, sorrow and sin. The man who has that idea is to be pitied. This world, which some think is heaven, has nothing in it to satisfy the soul. The more men see of it the less they think of it. They go all over it and then want to get out of it. Thousands every year commit suicide in order to get away from it.

Not only are the evidences and effects of sin all about us, but we find that sin abounds within us (Rom. 3:23). Surely we are not so blind as to imagine ourselves perfect. We might sooner number the grains of sand on the seashore than the iniquities of one man's life. Even if we could number man's sins, no one could estimate his *guilt*. In God's sight the guilt of one sin — and such a one as some foolishly call a little sin — merits His eternal displeasure (James 2: 10).

God's whole nature is turned in utter abhorrence against sin. He is immaculately pure and cannot be tempted with evil. In fact, if there is any difference in the attributes of God, that of His holiness seems to occupy first place. It is easy to comprehend the awfulness of sin when once we realize the moral perfection of God's holiness. His name is Holy, and He dwells in the high and holy place with only those who are holy.

God's Provision of a Holy Habitation (Ps. 47:8; 5:4; Isa. 63:15; Rev. 4)

Where does God dwell? We have already seen that God is omnipresent, but in His immeasurable dominion there is one place that could be called God's habitation. We learn from the Bible that there are three heavens: the first, as mentioned in the first chapter of Genesis, has reference to the immediate atmosphere serving the earth — the indispensable part of life; the second is the celestial heaven which includes not only the solar system, but the stars, constellations, and systems that constitute the boundless universe. But above all these and apart from them is the place reserved for the very special presence of God. Perhaps the most impressive description of the enthroned God in the presence of His worshipful attendants is in Revelation, chapter 4. Our limited senses as now constituted are too dull to comprehend the glory and majesty of this scene. In these headquarters of the immensity of creation, God dwells in a habitation of holiness.

Men who do not want to be holy on earth cannot hope to enter heaven. Even if they were admitted, they would not feel at home. As Whitefield, the great preacher, once declared, "The unholy man would be so unhappy in heaven that he would ask God to let him run down to hell for shelter." It is only those who "hunger and thirst after righteousness" that "shall be filled" with the happiness and holiness of heaven.

GOD'S JUSTICE

God's justice is the result of His holiness. While the righteousness of God may be said to be His love of holiness, the justice of God is His judgment of sin. This is seen in His:

Upholding Righteousness (Deut. 10:17, 18; Ps. 89:14; 97:2)

God's love of righteousness requires that there be absolute justice and unerring judgment in heaven. His clear sense of right and wrong will not permit Him to show any partiality. He is no respecter of persons, and cannot be bribed or influenced to do anything but what is absolutely just. He is the great champion of righteousness and justice.

Protecting the Righteous (Gen. 18:24-26; Ps. 96:11-13)

In order to uphold righteousness God must protect the righteous, those who have God's righteousness reckoned to them by believing on Jesus Christ (I Cor. 1:30; Rom. 10:10; Phil. 3:9), both in heaven and on earth. The day will come when the righteous will be separated from the *presence* of sin. In the meantime God protects them from the *power* of sin.

Abraham declared that the Judge of all the earth does right. This was proved in His protection of the righteous.

Lot (Gen. 18, 19; II Peter 2:7, 8)

Abraham's earnest prayer for his nephew was answered, not in the sparing of the intensely wicked city of Sodom as anticipated, but by the miraculous escape of Lot.

David (I Sam. 17:37)

Whether David was contending with a lion, or a bear, or the giant Goliath, his life was secure, because of God's protection.

Daniel (Dan. 6:22)

The safest place in Babylon for Daniel was in the lions' den, for he was assured of God's protection there as Shadrach, Meshach, and Abednego had been in the fiery furnace (Dan. 3:28).

Peter (Acts 12:11)

How peacefully Peter slept in the Jerusalem prison, although he was chained to four soldiers, and had been sentenced to be executed on the morrow. His life was preserved until his work was finished.

Paul (Acts 27:21-25)

The last chapters of Acts find Paul threatened by death again and again. Forty Jews took an oath that they would neither eat nor drink until they had slain the fearless apostle. The Roman government rescued and protected him, but this availed little when the terrible storm threatened to sink the ship and all its human cargo to the depths of the sea. Having escaped all this, his life was again in jeopardy when the deadly viper fastened itself on his hand. God needed Paul in Rome, and he was assured of His protection until he reached that city.

God not only protects righteous individuals, but also righteous nations. Again and again He protected His chosen people, Israel. In like manner He has protected His Church, and "the gates of hell shall not prevail against it" (Matt. 16:18).

Rewarding the Righteous (Ps. 11:4, 5, 7; Matt. 5:6; 13:43; Rom. 14:10; I Cor. 3:12-15; II Cor. 5:10; II Tim. 4:8)

The Lord is said to try or test out man's righteousness to see whether it is genuine. Happy indeed is the believer who desires righteousness and hates wickedness, for he shall be rewarded by an entrance into God's kingdom of righteousness. God has also promised a crown of righteousness to all who await with joy and expectation the coming of the righteous Judge to execute justice upon the earth. Here we are not always rewarded, but at the judgment seat of Christ we shall receive full reward for all the good we have done not for self-glory, but for Christ's glory. The righteousness of God is a guarantee of all this.

Punishing the Wicked (Ps. 7:11-17; 11:6; Matt. 25:46)

There is such a thing as the wrath of God. God is holy, infinitely holy, and He infinitely hates sin. We get glimpses of what God's hatred of sin must be in our own burning indignation at some outrage. But God's wrath at the smallest sin is infinitely greater than our anger at the most shocking crime. God must punish sin or He no longer can be God. If He tolerates sin or fails to punish the sinner, He must henceforth abdicate His throne of holiness and justice. The kindness of a king demands the punishment of those who are guilty. Even the wicked will admit the justice of their punishment.

There is no better illustration of this than the case of Pharaoh (Exod. 9:27). After the plague of hail, he sent for Moses and Aaron, and confessed, "I have sinned this time: the Lord is righteous, and I and my people are wicked." Pharaoh was not a repentant sinner. He later died in open rebellion against God. But Pharaoh here acknowledged the perfect justice of God in punishing him. And so it will be with every sinner at last. Every mouth will be stopped and all the world will become guilty before God (Rom. 3:19).

REVIEW QUESTIONS

1. With what two great distinguishing characteristics of God was Israel constantly impressed?
2. How is God's holiness taught in the Ten Commandments?
3. In what ways did the ceremonial law give instruction in holiness?
4. What three men had visions of God's holiness?
5. Give three illustrations of the punishment of profane men as evidence of God's holiness.
6. How does the provision of a Redeemer suggest God's holiness?
7. What do we mean by God's righteousness?
8. In what two ways did God show His righteousness?
9. What are the three heavens mentioned in Scripture?
10. What do we mean by God's justice?
11. In what four ways does God manifest His justice?
12. What five Bible characters illustrate God's protection of the righteous?

APPLYING DOCTRINE TO LIFE

1. How is the holiness, righteousness, and justice of God to be evidenced by the Spirit-filled teacher?
2. In what specific ways has your teaching been influenced by the fact of God's holiness?

THE TRUTHFULNESS, FAITHFULNESS, AND LOVE OF GOD

4

We have learned enough about the holiness and justice of God to realize it is impossible for sinners to dwell with a holy God nor escape the punishment of a just God. But apart from God's holiness and justice, there are other circumstances which positively assure us that the righteous shall be rewarded and the wicked punished. How do we know there is a heaven and a hell? *God's truthfulness, faithfulness, and love,* as we shall see, will prove the existence of these places.

> The heavens declare Thy glory, Lord
>> In every star Thy wisdom shines;
> But when our eyes behold Thy Word,
>> We read Thy name in every line.
> The rolling sun, the changing light,
>> And nights and days, Thy power confess;
> But the blest volume Thou didst write
>> Reveals Thy justice and Thy grace.
>
> — Isaac Watts

THE TRUTHFULNESS OF GOD

The truthfulness of God is evident from the following passages: Num. 23:19; Deut. 32:4; I Sam. 15:29; II Sam. 7:28; Ps. 146:6; Titus 1:2.

The Nature of God

God is not subject to those infirmities which lead men into falsehood. He "which keepeth truth forever" knows about deception and hypocrisy, so common to man. God cannot be guilty of deception, because:

He Is Too Wise To Be Untruthful

It is only a foolish man who lies. For some present advantage he may imagine the lie to be profitable, but sooner or later he will learn that "honesty is the best policy." The truth may suffer loss at first, but in the end it is triumphant, and true wisdom will prescribe honesty. Do you suppose God will choose the policy of the ignorant? Do you suppose that He who knows all things is not wise enough to choose the truth?

He Is Too Powerful To Be Untruthful

Someone has said that men find a lie "a present help in time of trouble," but when has God ever been in trouble? A man may lie to gain some present advantage, but when has God needed anything? He says, "Every beast of the forest is mine, and the cattle upon a thousand hills. I know all the fowls of the mountains and the wild beasts of the field are mine. If I were hungry, I would not tell thee: for the world is mine, and the fullness thereof" (Ps. 50:10-12). Men deceive to win honor and fame, but God needs no glory from His thankless creatures. To Him it is the greatest disgust of His righteous soul to be praised by unholy men. His glory is great enough, without stooping to lie for the respect and honor of men.

The Character of God

He Is Too Holy To Be Untruthful

Man is not a sinner because he is untruthful, but he is untruthful because he is a sinner. His tendency to deceive is due to his corrupt and depraved nature. But God is not man that He can lie. His absolute holiness prevents even the thought or the temptation to be untrue.

He Is Too Honorable To Be Untruthful (Heb. 6:13-18)

What in the above passages are the "two immutable things, in which it was impossible for God to lie"? The first of these is His divine integrity, of which we have just spoken. God prizes His integrity above all things. His word must be fulfilled at any cost, because His holy character will not permit otherwise. But the second unchangeable circumstance that makes it impossible for God to be untruthful is His oath. Here He is represented as confirming His promise to Abraham by an oath.

THE FAITHFULNESS OF GOD

The truthfulness of God is manifested in His faithfulness. In the very beginning of human history the devil insinuated that God was untruthful. What does the record say?

(Deut. 7:9; I Kings 8:56; Ps. 36:5; Lam. 3:23; I Cor. 1:9; I Thess. 5:24; Heb. 10:23)

God Has Been Faithful In His Promises

The Promise to Adam (Gen. 3:15; Gal. 4:4)

God warned Adam that if he ate of the forbidden fruit he would surely die. Satan declared that statement to be false; Adam would not die. But he did die spiritually the very moment he sinned, and by his death proved God true and Satan a liar. However, God gave the repentant Adam the promise of a Redeemer who would bruise the serpent's head, and His word was verified when Christ was born.

The Promises to Abraham (Gen. 15:13; Exod. 2:24)

God promised Abraham that He would make of him a great nation and that his descendants would possess the land in which he dwelt. For a period of four hundred years, however, his children would serve strangers and they would be in bondage and affliction until God would finally deliver them from their taskmasters. God heard the groaning of Israel in Egypt and remembered His covenant with Abraham.

The Promises to Moses (Exod. 3:12, 21; 4:12; 33:14)

God promised to be with Moses, to teach him what to say, to give the Israelites favor with the Egyptians, and an entrance into Canaan.

Moses reminded the Israelites in his farewell address of the long list of promises God made and kept with His people (Deut. 26: 7-9).

The Promise to Joshua (Josh. 1:1-5; 23:14)

God promised to be with Joshua as He was with Moses. So faithful was God in His dealing with this great military leader, that in his final message he declared that "not one thing hath failed of all the good things which the Lord your God spake concerning you; all are come to pass unto you, and not one thing hath failed thereof."

The Promise to David (II Sam. 7:8-16)

God promised that David's son, Solomon, should build the temple. Upon the dedication of that magnificent structure the great and wise king declared that there had not failed one word of all God's good promises which He had promised by the hand of Moses, His servant (I Kings 8:56).

God Has Been Faithful in His Judgments

History also records the fact that God has never failed to keep His word regarding judgment for sin. In every instance, unheeded warnings have been followed by punishment.

The Warning to the Antediluvians (Gen. 6:11-13; Luke 17:26, 27; II Pet. 2:5)

The great catastrophe which swept away the human race, with the exception of one family, proves that overwhelming numbers do not influence God's judgments. The unbelieving world perished as He said it would. The rainbow (Gen. 9:12-17) which God hung in the skies as the memorial of His promise never again to destroy the earth with a flood also proves that God cannot lie. There have been partial floods since then, but no world devastation such as Noah witnessed.

The Warning to Sodom (Gen. 18:20, 21; Luke 17:28, 29; II Pet. 2:6-8)

Lot was a silent missionary in the city of Sodom. His example was a warning against the wickedness of that city, but even his own family did not believe that God would destroy Sodom (Gen. 19:12-14). Had there been ten righteous people in Sodom, God would have kept His promise to Abraham to save the city (Gen.

18:32). But there were only four righteous ones, and God in His mercy saved them out of the doomed city (Gen. 19:16).

The Warning to Pharaoh (Exod. 5:1-3; Ps. 105:26-36)

Pharaoh was the mighty and haughty potentate of the greatest nation of ancient times. Why should he pay any attention to the Lord — a tribal god, as he supposed? But Pharaoh learned that the God of Israel was the God of heaven and earth, who executeth judgments according to His decree. Study the ten plagues and their advance announcements to see how accurately God kept His word.

The Warning to Israel (Deut. 7:6-11; Jer. 25:4-11)

Again and again God's chosen people were warned by faithful prophets, "rising early and speaking," that they would lose their liberty and their land if they did not repent of their national sins and return unto the Lord. And though Israel was His "peculiar treasure" and dearly loved for the faith of their fathers, yet God punished His children.

The Warning to Nineveh and Babylon

Two prophets, Nahum and Habakkuk, wrote exclusively about the impending doom of these majestic and magnificent cities of ancient days. At the time, they were in the height of their power, and nothing seemed further remote than their destruction. Ask the wastes of Nineveh; turn to the mounds of Babylon! We may boldly ask the traveler, "Hath he said, and hath he not done it? Has God's curse been an idle word? Have His words fallen to the ground?"

THE LOVE OF GOD

The Apostle John, through the Spirit of God, penned for us some of the most profound insights into the nature of God in remarkably short statements: God is spirit (John 4:24), God is light (I John 1:5), and God is love (I John 4:8). Of all the characteristics of the divine nature, none moves the human heart nor reaches man's deepest need more than love. Small wonder that John 3:16 has been the favorite text for multitudes of believers. That verse magnifies not the infinite wisdom, absolute power, nor immaculate holiness of God, but the greatness of His love.

Whom Does God Love?

His Son (Matt. 3:17; 17:5; Mark 1:11; 9:7; Luke 9:35; 20:13; John 5:20; 15:9; 17:24)

Every time the voice from heaven witnessed to the fact that Jesus was the Christ, it spoke of Him as the *beloved* Son. At the baptism and again at the transfiguration we hear this expression of endearment, as well as testimony of approval. Christ also referred to the love of the Father for Him, in speaking both to the unbelieving Jews and to the sympathetic disciples.

"In the beginning God created the heaven," but the day that He began to love the Son was long before this. Of course, if the love of God is eternal, as His very nature requires, then that love must have had an eternal object to love. So Christ in addressing the Father says, "Thou lovedst me before the foundation of the world" (John 17:24).

His Children (Deut. 7:6-8; John 14:21-23; 16:27; 17:23; I John 3:1, 2)

Moses declared that God had chosen Israel above all the peoples that were on the earth, not because of their numbers, or any commendable characteristic, but because He loved them. Moreover, He loved them because He first loved Abraham, Isaac, and Jacob, their fathers (Deut. 4:37), and was keeping His covenant with them.

In His farewell address, Christ had much to say about the love of the Father for the Son, but He reached the climax when He said, "He that loveth me shall be loved of my Father." Three times He compared the Father's love for the disciples with God's love for the Son. If we truly believe these words, we shall realize that we are not on the outskirts of God's love, but in its very midst. There stands Christ in the very center of God's love, and He draws us to Himself that we might enjoy the same warmth of love that the Father lavishes upon Him.

What honor that in this incalculable, incomprehensible universe there should be found intelligent beings so highly honored as to be called sons of God! Wherever this term is found in the Old Testament, invariably it refers to the angels. When we think of the majesty of these celestial, eternal creatures, we are not surprised that they are called the sons of God. The marvel is that this term should now be associated with such vastly subordinate creatures as constitute the human race. No wonder the apostle cried, "Behold what manner of love the Father hath bestowed upon us that *we* should be called the sons of God." Sons of God! Heirs of glory! Princes of supreme sovereignty! Participants of endless bliss!

His Enemies (John 3:16; Rom. 5:8)

"For God so loved the world" was a startling truth to Nicodemus, who thought God was concerned only about the Jews. God loved not the Jew only, but also the Gentile; not a part of the world, but every man in it, irrespective of his moral character.

God takes no pleasure in the death of His enemies, but is "longsuffering to usward, not willing that any should perish, but that all should come to repentance" (II Pet. 3:9). Christ's mission to this earth was for the rebellious sinner — "While we were yet sinners, Christ died for us." Thus God commended His love toward wayward ones.

How Does God Love?

By His Goodness (Ps. 25:8; 33:5; 34:8; 65:9; 68:19; 119:68; 145:7; Matt. 5:45; Acts 14:17)

The smiles of God's benevolence are upon all creation. God's hand feeds all His creatures. He sweetens the clover top to the cattle's taste; provides the mountain stream from which the deer may drink; pours nectar into the cup of the honeysuckle to refresh the hummingbird; and spreads a banquet of blossoms for the honeybee.

And how good God is to the human race! The necessities of life are provided in abundance. Man has all the air and all the water he needs; the heat and light of the glorious sunshine are provided — all without money and without price. We are created amid conditions that are just suited to our life and fitted to make us happy. The light is suited to the eye, the ear to the atmosphere.

By His Discipline (Prov. 3:12; Heb. 12:6-11; Rev. 3:19)

God cares enough for His children to guide them and correct them. Earth is not our permanent home. It is only a place in which we are being prepared for a future state. School is good for a child, although the study may at times be irksome. The discipline of suffering is good for man, although at the time it is not joyous but grievous. Men have said, "If God would only tell me that He loves me!" Well, if He has sent you sorrow or pain, He has told you that He loves you. "Happy is the man whom God correcteth." This is a deep, reassuring truth, that He orders each particular blow, or weight, or sorrow, or fretting care, or harassing discomfort or unrest, in His all-wise love, fitting each trial to our own particular temperament. It is not merely an all-wise God, unseen, unfelt, at a distance, who guides all things in perfect wisdom for the good of each individual creature which He has made. Rather God manifests individual, infinite, personal love. He who loves us infinitely, loves us individually.

By His Mercy (Deut. 4:31; Ps. 86:5; 103:8, 17, 18; 145:8, 9; II Pet. 3:9)

Mercy is kindness for the miserable — pity, compassion, forbearance, gentleness. It is synonymous with the term "loving-kindness," so frequently found in Scripture. Loving-kindness is that attribute of God which leads Him to bestow upon His obedient children constant and choice blessings. "He that trusteth in the Lord, mercy shall compass him about" (Ps. 32:10). This act of trust on the part of the believer protects him just as in the case of a parent and a child. The moment we throw ourselves on God, we are enveloped in His mercy. Mercy is our environment and protects us like a fiery wall, so that no evil can break through. God's mercy is seen too, not only in healing the sick in answer to prayer when it is His will to do so (Phil. 2:27), but also in comforting sorrowing loved ones (II Cor. 1:4).

Mercy is exercised also toward the disobedient, by long-suffering and forbearance. If God should deal with them in justice, they would be cut off immediately. "Nevertheless for thy great mercies' sake thou didst not utterly consume them; nor forsake them: for thou art a gracious and merciful God" (Neh. 9:31). "It is because of the Lord's mercies that we are not consumed" (Lam. 3:22). The sinner is already condemned, but God in mercy is seemingly reluctant to carry out the sentence. He spares him as long as it is right that a condemned man should live. It was through His mercy that God spared Sodom until Lot could escape. It was by His mercy that the Canaanites were permitted to live four hundred years after their land had been given to Abraham for a possession. God is slow to execute sentence, even when He has declared it.

By His Grace (Ps. 84:11; Acts 11:20-23; 13:43; Rom. 3:24, 25; I Tim. 1:14)

Grace is unmerited favor. It is unexpected love exercised toward the unworthy. Mercy is the term more frequently used in the Old Testament, since God's loving-kindness was primarily exercised toward His chosen people Israel. Grace, on the other hand, is emphasized in the New Testament, since the term receives its largest use in expressing God's unmerited favor to the Gentiles. God showed mercy to Israel because of His covenant with Abraham, but He showed grace to those who had no claims on Him. When the disobedient Jews claimed their rights as children of Abraham, John the Baptist declared that God could raise up children out of stones (Matt. 3:9). Even the Jews, under the terms of the old covenant, were not justified by works or covenant rights, but by the grace of God expressed in the atonement of His beloved Son (Rom. 3:21-25). God showed His regard for Israel by giving the nation His law, and His mercy to those that disobeyed as well as obeyed it, but *grace* and truth came by Jesus Christ (John 1:17).

The Grace of God (II Cor. 8:9; Eph. 1:7).

The grace of our Lord Jesus Christ was expressed by the fact that "though he was rich, yet for your sakes he became poor, that ye through his poverty might become rich." The riches of God's grace were expressed by the forgiveness of our sins, by redemption through the blood of Christ. Grace was God's disrobing Himself of all His splendor, and coming down to the earth as an unwelcome guest to show His love for a rebellious people (Phil. 2:5-8). Grace is God dressed in the crimson robes of a dying Redeemer, courting the love of the unholy and unlovely. Grace is God's laying aside

His glory that He might express His abhorrence of man's sin by enduring its penalties instead of inflicting them. Grace is God's following the unbeliever through life, exhibiting His wounded hands and feet to prove and plead His love. Grace is the Good Shepherd going out into the wilderness after the wayward sheep before there is any alarm felt because of its danger or any desire on its part to return.

The Riches of God's Grace (Eph. 2:4-7)

The riches of God's grace included not only the condescension and redemption of the Lord Jesus Christ, but the resurrection, exaltation, and glorification of the humble believer. Grace is so amazing, so marvelous, that it will be the theme of admiration and wonder in the ages to come. It is only when we understand something of the greatness of God — his greatness in power and pomp and possessions — that we can realize something of the riches of His grace in giving such insignificant, unworthy, and even rebellious creatures, the unmerited privilege of sharing His glory (Tit. 3:3-7). The song of heaven, the hymn of eternity, will be the song of the redeemed, rejoicing in the grace of God (Rev. 5:9, 10).

REVIEW QUESTIONS

1. Prove the truthfulness of God by His nature.
2. How does the character of God guarantee His truthfulness?
3. Give five illustrations of God's faithfulness in His promises.
4. Give five illustrations which prove God has been faithful in His judgments.
5. How did God fulfill His promise to Adam?
6. How was God's faithfulness seen in the deluge?
7. Why is the love of God said to be the greatest of all His attributes?
8. Whom does God love?
9. What Bible passages teach of God's love for His children?
10. How do we know that God loves His enemies?
11. How does God love?
12. What was the grace of God in Jesus Christ?

APPLYING DOCTRINE TO LIFE

1. How is the truthfulness, faithfulness, and love of God to be evidenced by the Spirit-filled teacher?
2. Compare the relative importance of God's faithfulness and yours in the ministry of teaching.

THE WORKS OF GOD

5

Psalm 19 proclaims that God is the author of two books — the book of nature and the book of His own self revelation, the Word of God. The book of nature is a large and fascinating volume containing many chapters such as astronomy, geology, and botany. To master the content of any one of these would require years. Our concern, however, is to study God's work of creation in the light of biblical knowledge. Eight characteristics of creation will be noted. These not only witness to the handiwork of the Creator, but also represent some attribute of His divine nature.

GOD'S WORK OF CREATION

"God's work of creation is the making of all things out of nothing by the word of His power in the space of six days and all very good."

Method of Creation — The Power of God (Ps. 33:6-9; 115:3; Jer. 10: 12, 13)

"And God said" introduces nine verses of the creation chapter (Gen. 1). It was the infinite power of God that gave His word immediate obedience. "He spake and it was done" (Ps. 33:9). No waiting millions of years for some tedious process of evolution. God's power produced immediate and complete results.

The fallacy of the evolutionary theory lies in the fact that men arrive at conclusions by inferences drawn from facts. The truth is that the similarity between men and other species merely proves a common creator, not a common ancestor; a common author, not a common derivation. Works of art by the same artist are usually recognized because of similarities. But the real marvel of creation is the diversity and not the resemblance of its constituent parts. Man's inventions need to be patented to prevent reproduction, so prone is human nature to copy; but the Master Mind is inexhaustible in its types and patterns.

Plan of Creation — The Wisdom of God (Job 26:7; 36:26-29; 38:36-41; Ps. 40:5; 95:5; 104:24; Prov. 3:19)

In Job we read of the marvel of gravitation and "the balancing of the clouds." Life is possible upon this globe only because of its atmosphere and its proper distance from the sun. How is the latter maintained? By gravitation, an invisible cable 5,000 miles in diameter and 93,000,000 miles in length. To prepare a connection of such vast proportions is beyond the resources of man; even if it were completed, he would not have the power to attach it to the sun.

The divine wisdom in planning the system for watering the earth is equally marvelous. Three-fourths of the earth's surface is water. But how can it be liberated from its saline impurities and carried to the parched portions of the earth? Who that had never before seen a cloud or a shower could have solved this problem? The efficient plan conceived by the Great Engineer would never have entered the human mind. And how can these tons upon tons of water, purified and elevated, be sustained without destructive discharge upon the earth? Had not God in His wisdom put a check on rainfall, every rain cloud, with its devastating dangers, would be an object of terror to all who behold it.

Perfection of Original Creation — The Holiness of God (Gen. 1:31; Deut. 32:4; Isa. 45:18; Jer. 4:23-26)

Why should not a perfect God create a perfect universe? He must be perfect in Himself and, therefore, He could not create anything imperfect. In fact, we are told that "God saw everything that he had made, and, behold, it was very good." There is not a suggestion in the Bible that anything that came from the hands of God was imperfect. Instead we find the word "good" and "very good" used again and again to denote the perfection of His work.

God gave Job to understand (Job 38:4-7) that when He created the earth it was so marvelously perfect that "the morning stars sang together, and the sons of God shouted for joy." Do you suppose that these highly intelligent angels shouted over a chaotic mass such as our evolutionists would have us think originally constituted the earth? No, it was a beautiful world, a perfect creation, that called forth the Creator's praise on the morning of creation.

Vastness of Creation — The Immensity of God (Job 22:12; Ps. 8:3, 4; 92:5; 145:3; Rev. 15:3)

Job's would-be comforter, Eliphaz, recognized thousands of years ago that the stars were inconceivably remote. The sun and its system of planets is a very minute part of the millions of orbs that constitute our universe. Our Milky Way galaxy is only one of many galaxies that cover space, each one with a retinue of countless billions of stars. In fact, we do not know the confines of this vast universe or how many stars there are. Though men have made great advances into space, they acknowledge that creation is immeasurable and well-nigh incomprehensible. No wonder an eminent American astronomer exclaimed, "Our greatest debt to astronomy is that it has shown us what a vast thing creation is, and what a small part of the Creator's work is this little earth upon which we live." God Himself best describes the vastness of His creation, for it was He who "meted out heaven with the span, and comprehended the dust of the earth in a measure, and weighed the mountains in scales, and the hills in a balance . . ." (Isa. 40:12).

Regularity in Creation — The Unchangeableness of God (Gen. 8:22; Job 38:37; Ps. 74:16, 17; Eccles. 1:5-7)

In the memory of man has the return of the seasons ever failed, or the day ceased to follow the night? In some places on the earth the recurring rains come with such regularity during the rainy seasons that it is said one can "set his watch by the time of occurrence of the daily thunderstorm." People who insist that a permanent change in climate has taken place during their lifetime are in error. We have learned from a study of statistics that wet and dry, cold and hot periods come in cycles. Planets and their moons move with such regularity that we can determine eclipses to a minute a thousand years hence; sunspot periods reoccur in cycles; and stars proceed on their charted courses with a changeless velocity. Some of the stars fluctuate in brightness, going through a period of sudden rise of brilliancy, and then slowly falling to dimness, in time ranging from a few hours to fifty days. Such system and regularity speak of the unchangeableness of God.

Variety in Creation — The Exhaustlessness of God (Job 38:22; Isa. 40:26, 28; I Cor. 15:41)

None of the planets is like another and "one star differeth from another in glory." It is estimated that in our galaxy alone there are enough stars for every one of the billions of people of the earth to be given hundreds of stars to rule. And yet these gigantic suns so differ from one another in distance, diameter, direction, velocity, and substance that God "called them all by names by the greatness of his might." Could we ever count the leaves on the trees? Could we even estimate the number in a single forest? And yet no two leaves are exactly alike, although they may have enough in common to classify them. Botanists have identified more than a third of a million different species of plants. We are bewildered at the thought of the countless variety of sizes, forms, and colors which such a vast host exhibit, and overwhelmed at the discovery that even the individuals of the same species differ. There are about five thousand species of grass and no two blades of the same species are alike. Who can count the snowflakes? We cannot count them. However, we can catch some and examine these marvels of nature. While we would observe that they always show six sides, their variations seem unlimited and no two designs appear alike.

Usefulness in Creation — The Goodness of God (Deut. 8:7-9; Job 37:17; Matt. 5:45; Acts 14:17)

Every green blade that springs from the ground is a magazine of contrivances; every leaf serves a definite purpose. Have we ever realized how lavishly God has provided in creation for the necessities of life? Men could not live an hour without air or water, and scarcely exist without the heat and light of the sun. But there is an abundant supply of all of these vital commodities provided without money and without price. Even when economic recessions and depressions have come, they were not occasioned by man's lack of any of life's essentials. Man's difficulties come about through a scarcity of money, the love of which, the Bible tells us, is the "root of all evil" (I Tim. 6:10). God has provided the human race with vast resources in productive soil, recurring showers, and stimulating sunshine. Our debt to nature is far greater than most men imagine. It has been estimated that after the average man has deducted the contribution of nature and the contribution of society toward the production of his commodity, he will find that he has not put more than two and one-half per cent into it himself.

Purpose in Creation — The Glory of God (Ps. 19:1; 145:10; Prov. 16:4; Isa. 44:24; Rom. 11:36; Col. 1:16; Rev. 4:11)

"All things were created by him and for him." Whatever we have is from God and should be used and employed for Him. We should use all things with due thankfulness to the generous Giver, employing them in our service soberly and wisely, considering they stand related to God as their Creator, and are His workmanship.

Truly man's chief end, like that of all other creatures, is to glorify God and enjoy Him forever. We cannot enjoy God unless we recognize His sovereignty and proprietorship in all the wonderful things which He has made for His honor and glory, as well as for our pleasure.

GOD'S WORK OF PROVIDENCE

Little things that have determined lives and shaped the destiny of nations are not accidents. They constitute the evidence that God is directing the affairs of this world. While His greatness is unsearchable and the immensity of His creation incomprehensible, nevertheless, He is interested in all His creatures and all their actions. God's provision for His creatures and His protection and guidance of them are called the *works of providence*. These are even greater evidences of His existence, greater instructors of His character, and greater marvels of His nature than the works of creation. Men who cannot see God in creation can hardly fail to recognize Him in His works of providence.

Providential Provision (Deut. 8:3, 4, 15, 16; Job 38:41; Ps. 65:9-13; 104:10-16, 21, 27, 28; Matt. 6:26; Acts 14:17)

Psalm 104 is a eulogy of God's marvelous provision for His creatures. Water is the great necessity of the animal world. A horse can live twenty-five days on water, but only five days when food is provided without water. However, the Creator has interspersed springs, creeks, and waterways among the hills where there is good pasturage to be found. "They give drink to every beast of the field: the wild asses quench their thirst. By them shall the fowls have their habitation." In time these watercourses would run dry, so "he watereth the hills from his chambers," and the refreshing rainfall "causeth the grass to grow for the cattle, and herb for the service of man: that he may bring food out of the earth." Not only the domestic animals, but "the young lions roar after their prey, and seek their meat from God." Even the innumerable creatures of the ocean wait upon God, that He may give them their meat in due season.

Much of the animal world makes no provision for the future. The ravens neither sow nor reap, neither have storehouse nor barn, "and God feedeth them." Experience has taught them that God will provide faithfully and abundantly. If God cares for the birds, how much more will He care for us? The value of the sparrow of which our Lord spoke (Matt. 10:29) is just about as little as anything that could come under appraisement. Two of them were sold for a farthing, which is less than a penny in our currency. Moreover, these common birds which have neither song nor plummage are the least desirable of the winged creatures. In many places they are regarded as a nuisance, fit only for food for the other creatures. Yet God cares for them!

> Said the robin to the sparrow,
>   "I should really like to know,
> Why these anxious human beings
>   Rush about and worry so?"
> Said the sparrow to the robin,
>   "Friend, I think that it must be
> That they have no heavenly Father
>   Such as cares for you and me."

God's gracious provision for mankind is seen in the remarkable capacity most plants have to reproduce. The common cereals often yield from sixty to one hundredfold. One castor oil plant will produce fifteen hundred, and one sunflower four thousand seeds in a single season. From one grain of corn, if it and all its produce were from year to year planted and duly cultivated in favorable soil and climate, sufficient seed might be raised in five years to plant hills of corn with three grains in every yard of dry land upon the face of the globe. In the creative fiat, "Let the earth bring forth grass, the herb yielding seed . . . after its kind," God made abundant provision, not only to perpetuate vegetation, but also to meet the wants of all His creatures. Poverty is not the institution of heaven. The causes lie with men.

Not only does God make general provision for all mankind, but He especially cares for the needs of His children. When the chosen people were in the barren wilderness of the Sinai peninsula, special arrangements were necessary to feed a multitude of two million men, women, and children. The manna which was supplied day by day for forty years met every requirement. It was pleasant to the taste, it was nourishing, and there was sufficient for all. This miracle, not only of food, but also of clothes (Deut. 8:3, 4) is an irrefutable proof of all the Bible assumes concerning the personality, love, and power of God, as well as His faithfulness and deep concern for all His children. The murmurings and dissatisfaction of the Israelites concerning the manna teach lessons of great value to us. "Man did eat angels' food" (Ps. 78:25), and his dissatisfaction with it revealed a rebellious nature which would be unhappy in heaven.

Providential Protection

Psalm 91 is a eulogy of God's marvelous protection of His children — those that dwell "in the secret place of the most High." Because He hath set His love upon thee, "he shall give his angels charge over thee, to keep thee in all thy ways." Christ spoke of the guardian angels of children (Matt. 18:10), and older ones are assured that these heavenly beings are surrounding and protecting them (Heb. 1:14). Protection is afforded against harm and disease.

Against Harm (Ps. 34:7; 41:2; 91:5; 125:2; II Kings 6:14-17; II Chron. 16:9; Zech. 2:5; Luke 21:18)

You will remember how God protected Elisha when the entire Syrian army came to capture the prophet. For months this man of God had been revealing the Syrian war plans to the king of Israel. Now the Syrian host of horses and chariots and infantry surrounded the city in which the prophet resided. What a terrible sight greeted the eye of the prophet's servant the next morning — a vast army seeking the life of one man! In his terror he cried, "Alas, my master! What shall we do?" "Fear not," said Elisha, "for they that be with us are more than they which be with them."

Impossible? Perhaps to those who know nothing about the providence of God! Elisha's servant was such an one, and so the prophet prayed that his eyes might be opened to see the heavenly host that covered the mountains to protect him from the Syrian army. Such is the divine protection God affords His children.

Against Disease (Deut. 7:15; Exod. 15:26; Ps. 91:6, 10)

"What is your life?" Well does the writer of old answer the question, "It is even a vapor that appeareth for a little time, and then vanisheth away" (James 4:14). Your own breath is a picture of the flimsy thing which men call life.

Justinian, an emperor of Rome, died by going into a room which had been newly painted; Adrian, a pope, was strangled to death by a fly. There are a thousand gates to death. Men have been choked by a grape seed, carried off by a whiff of foul air. Germs of fatal diseases are all about us. It is only God's providence that keeps us from contracting all the diseases with which we come in contact. God is taking better care of us than we can take of ourselves. His care exceeds that of the dearest friends and the best physicians. Look at a mother. How careful she is! If her child has a little cough, she notices it; the slightest weakness is sure to be observed. But she has never thought of numbering the hairs of her child's head. The absence of two or three of them would give her no concern. However, God is so careful of us that He numbers the hairs on our heads (Matt. 10:30).

Against Evil (Ps. 91:10; 121:3-8; I Cor. 10:13)

Psalm 121 is the Traveler's Psalm. In some homes this Scripture is read when some member of the family is about to go on a journey. It is not so much a prayer as a meditation upon God's providence. "He that keepeth thee will not slumber." His protecting care not only keeps from harm, but from evil too. "The Lord shall preserve thee from all evil: he shall preserve thy soul."

Have we ever considered how frequently God's providence has protected us in times of temptation? Providence has not permitted the temptation to come at times when we would have been overwhelmed by it. At other times when the temptation has come, God has providentially given us supernatural strength to resist it. With the temptation there has been provided a way of escape, so we are able to bear it. Strange it is, but many a man's character has been saved by God's providence. The best man that ever lived little knows how much he owes for preservation to this providence, another aspect of God's grace. He has not led us into temptation, but has delivered us from evil.

Providential Guidance (Gen. 45:7; Esther 4:14; Ps. 37:5, 23-25; Dan. 2:21)

Psalm 37 is called the "Fret Not Psalm." Not only are its forty verses introduced by the two words, "Fret not," but its entire content speaks of God's providential direction of the lives of those that trust in Him. The good man is exhorted to commit his way unto the Lord, trust also in Him, and He shall bring it to pass. God has a plan for each child of His and will guide him and direct him once he is surrendered.

Joseph was fully surrendered to God's program for his life, although he little knew what God intended to do with him. God had in mind that Joseph should be governor of Egypt. How was this to be done? The first thing was that Joseph's brethren must hate him. Next they must put him into a pit. Why was he not killed? Why was Reuben delayed in rescuing him? Because God planned to have the Ishmaelites come along at the right moment and purchase him. Why were the Ishmaelites going to Egypt? Why did they sell Joseph to Potiphar? Why was Joseph falsely accused and thrown into prison? How was it that both the butler and the baker offended the king? Why did they both dream? Why did they happen to ask Joseph to interpret their dreams? Why did the butler, when released, forget all about Joseph? Why did Pharaoh dream? These are all the connecting links of providence. If Joseph had not been put into the pit he would never have been the servant of Potiphar; if he had never been thrown into prison he never would have interpreted the butler's dream, and if Pharaoh had not dreamed, Joseph would never have been sent for. As someone has said, "God put Joseph into prison so Pharaoh could find him when he wanted him." How well Joseph recognized this providential leading is indicated by his statement to his brethren, "Be not grieved that ye sold me thither, for God did send me before you to preserve life."

REVIEW QUESTIONS

1. What was the method of creation?
2. What was the plan of creation?
3. How do we know that the original creation was perfect?
4. How does astronomy corroborate the Bible in revealing the vastness of creation?
5. Contrast regularity with the variety in creation.
6. What Scripture passages declare the purpose in creation?
7. What do we mean by the works of providence?
8. Give some illustrations of God's providential provisions.
9. What do God's providential provisions reveal about His nature?
10. In what three ways does God exercise His providential protection?
11. How is Psalm 37 true today for the believer in experiencing God's providential direction?
12. In what ways was the providence of God evidenced in Joseph's life?

APPLYING DOCTRINE TO LIFE

1. How would you witness to an unbeliever concerning the question of evolution vs. God's creative work by His Word?
2. What part does the teacher's ministry have in the effects of God's providential care?

THE PREEXISTENCE AND INCARNATION OF CHRIST

6

The question for today is not, "Did Christ live?" There is too much established evidence to question the fact that He lived. The keystone of Christianity is Jesus Christ. No other man occupies the same position with regard to any religion that Christ occupies in regard to Christianity. He is at once its founder and its subject. Jesus Christ is the great figure of the centuries and every system of theology and philosophy must take account of Him. Men may oppose Him and reject His claim, but they cannot ignore Him.

THE PREEXISTENCE OF CHRIST

The perennial question, then, for every man, woman and child, where "the name that is above every name" has gone is, "What think ye of Christ?" Whose son is He?" A man's parentage ordinarily makes very little difference to us. He rises or falls according to his own ability and efficiency. Our estimate of Shakespeare or Lincoln is no greater because we know their ancestry. But it is different with Jesus Christ. His practical relationship to the world is bound up in His origin. His life suggests and His words lay claim to a superhuman lineage. He did not acknowledge Joseph, the carpenter of Nazareth, as His father. His sinless life and the far-reaching accomplishments of His death are grounded in the fact of His eternal preexistence.

Evidence of the Preexistent Christ

Personal Testimony

There are numerous New Testament witnesses to a preexisting Christ.

Christ (John 6:32-38, 41-50)

Probably the greatest gathering our Lord ever addressed was the occasion when His prolonged message and ministry prompted the feeding of the hungry thousands. He used this widely recognized miracle to press home the truth that He was the Bread of Life which had come down from heaven. When the Jews objected to this extraordinary claim, contending that they knew His father and mother, He ignored their arguments and once more reiterated that He was the Living Bread from heaven, and therefore greater than the heavenly manna which had supplied their temporal needs.

Peter (I Pet. 1:19, 20)

Outstanding among the disciples was Peter. Not only did he

write two Epistles and contribute to the preparation of a Gospel, but his name is found more frequently in the New Testament than that of any other human character. He believed in the preexistence of Christ, for he declares that He "was foreordained before the foundation of the world, but was manifest in these last times."

John the Baptist (John 1:27-30)

John the Baptist was the most popular preacher of his day. He was the most discussed man of the hour, for there went out to hear him the multitudes from "Jerusalem, and all Judea, and all the region round about Jordan" (Matt. 3:5). Yet he was constantly referring to a far greater person who was to come after him. He declared, "After me cometh a man which is preferred before me: for he was before me." In other words, he used the fact of Christ's preexistence as the argument for His superiority to himself.

John the Apostle (John 1:1, 2, 18; I John 1:1, 2)

Instead of opening his narrative with the ministry of Christ or tracing His genealogy from Adam or Abraham, John pushes back His existence to the beginning of all beginnings. The genesis of the first book in the Bible is, "In the beginning God," and the genesis of the fourth Gospel is, "In the beginning was the Word." God, then, and the Word must have coexisted in the very beginning. And what John declares in his Gospel he also records in his first Epistle. To his mind it was a marvelous privilege to have actually seen and heard and touched the one and only Eternal Being.

Paul (I Cor. 8:6; II Tim. 1:9)

It was a vision of the risen Christ which converted the greatest of Jewish scholars and transformed him from Saul the cruel persecutor to Paul the heroic missionary. Yet Paul also seems to have had a full realization of the preexistence of Christ, for he declares that "he is before all things, and by him all things consist" (Col. 1:17).

Prophetic Witnesses

Not only are there New Testament but also Old Testament witnesses to a preexisting Christ.

David (Ps. 40:6-8; Heb. 10:5-10)

David was permitted to draw aside the curtain of time and clearly see the crucifixion of Christ one thousand years ahead of time (Ps. 22). But he was also permitted to look back into the council of eternity. He saw that majestic scene of God the Father, God the Son, and God the Holy Spirit discussing the salvation of a sin-cursed world. No burnt offerings or sacrifices would suffice for its salvation. None but a sinless being could be accepted to atone for guilt-stained creatures. Who then could go? The Holy One of God. Who then would go? Listen! It is the voice of God the Son who speaks: "Lo, I come to do thy will, O God."

Micah (Mic. 5:2)

The prophets were not only given details of our Lord's earthly advent, but it also appears that they too recognized His preexistence. In announcing that Bethlehem would be the birthplace of the Messiah of Israel, the prophet Micah strikingly adds that He was to be One "whose goings forth have been from of old, from everlasting."

Eternity of the Preexistent Christ

Not only is there trustworthy evidence of the preexistence of Christ, but there also is testimony to the fact that He shared the eternity of God.

The One Ever-Present (John 8:56-58)

When Moses asked for a message to prove that he was God's ambassador, he was told to declare to the children of Israel that "I AM hath sent me unto you" (Exod. 3:13, 14). This is another way of declaring that with God there is neither past nor future, but an eternal present. When the Jews argued with Christ that He was not yet fifty years old and therefore could not possibly have seen Abraham, His memorable reply was, "Before Abraham was, I am." When the writer to the Hebrews asserted that our Lord was a priest after the order of Melchisedec rather than of Aaron, it was only to claim for Him an existence which had "neither beginning of days, nor end of life" (Heb. 7:3).

The Alpha and Omega (Heb. 13:8; Rev. 1:8; 22:13)

The preexistence as well as the immutability of our Lord was declared in that brief and striking statement, "Jesus Christ the same yesterday, and today, and forever." At the beginning and again at the end of the revelation of Jesus Christ which was given to His servant at Patmos, John was told to write, "I am Alpha and Omega, the first and the last." This is a clear testimony to His eternal preexistence.

Adoration of the Preexistent Christ

Before our Lord became flesh and dwelt among men, He existed in a state of glory and was an object of worship.

Worship (Heb. 1:4-6, 13, 14)

While on earth, our Lord was accorded worship (Matt. 2:11; 14:33; 28:9; Luke 24:52), and it is noteworthy that He never protested against it. Long before this, however, He was the object of worship by the angels. He was higher than they; "He had obtained a more excellent name than they," for He was the Father's Son and occupied the place of honor by His side.

Glory (John 1:14; 17:5, 24)

The glory of God implies the full expression of God's life, all its beauty, purity, holiness, majesty, power and other attributes in manifestation. We might say that Christ's cloak of humanity which

He wore while on earth was a mantle covering the glory to which He was accustomed at all other times. The transfiguration of which all the Gospel writers speak (John 1:14) was that brief removal of His earthly garment which the three privileged disciples witnessed on the Mount of Transfiguration (Matt. 17:1-5).

At the close of His earthly ministry, our Lord concluded His valediction with an intercessory prayer in which He requested that the disciples might behold the glory which He shared with God "before the world was." Twice He made this petition, reiterating His preexistence by adding, "Thou lovedst me before the foundation of the world" (John 17:24).

Activities of the Preexistent Christ

The preexistence of Christ is further revealed by the work attributed to Him. His was not an inactive existence, but one in which He shared the activities of the Father and the Holy Spirit.

Creator (John 1:3; Col. 1:16-18; Heb. 1:2, 10; 2:10)

In a former lesson we attempted to fathom the greatness of God's creation, a work that is immeasurable and well-nigh incomprehensible. We were amazed and awed not only by its immensity but by its perfection, its variety, and its utility. And yet we need to be reminded that our Lord and Savior Jesus Christ shared in all this mighty and marvelous work, and that "all things were made by him; and without him was not anything made that was made" (John 1:3). His activities not only included the visible universe of galaxies, but the invisible principalities and heavenly thrones (Col. 1:16), which may be far more marvelous and majestic than that which mortal eye can discern. Moreover, all these wonderful works were not only made by Him, but also for Him (Col. 1:16; Heb. 2:10).

Controller (Col. 1:17; Heb. 1:3)

We have studied about the providential provision, protection, and guidance afforded God's creatures. We learned for our comfort and assurance that God controls not only the movements of the heavenly bodies, but the destinies of the nations. But this great task of governing and sustaining the universe and all creatures, human and angelic, is a work of God the Son fully as much as of God the Father. Jesus demonstrated this by His miracles when He was on earth, for the winds and waves obeyed Him, and the demons were subject to His command. Long before this, He controlled the planets in their orbits and He ordained and sustained their fields of gravitation.

THE INCARNATION OF CHRIST

The word "incarnation" comes from the Latin, and literally means "embodiment, or the assumption of humanity." That He whom the heaven of heavens cannot contain should voluntarily imprison Himself upon a mere particle of His immeasurable creation; that He whose brilliant majesty is brighter than the sun should cover His glory with the cloak of human flesh is inconceivable, and well-nigh unbelievable, were it not for the facts which plainly testify to its truth.

Human Parentage

Genealogies (Matt. 1:1; Luke 3:23-38)

The human ancestry of Christ is traced by two of the Gospel writers. Matthew opens his narrative with a genealogy to prove that Jesus Christ as the son of David was heir to the throne of Israel, and as the son of Abraham was the child of promise in whom all families of the earth were to be blessed. Luke does not stop at David or Abraham, but goes back to the first man, who was the father of Jews and Gentiles alike.

Born of a Woman (Matt. 1:18-20; Luke 1:26-35; John 1:14; Gal. 4:4)

Not only do we have the express statement to this fact in the Acts and the Epistles, but the Gospel writers provide the details. Both Matthew and Luke testify that this birth was different from all ordinary births. Joseph, we are told, was engaged but not yet married to Mary, and naturally was deeply grieved when he was led to believe that the young girl he loved had been unfaithful to him. Perhaps as he lay awake at night, trying to plan some way of putting her away privately to save her from death — which was the penalty of the Jewish law — an angel appeared to him and explained the creative act whereby God broke through the chain of human generation and brought into the world a supernatural being. We read that Joseph accepted the explanation and that his marriage to Mary was not consummated until after Jesus was born. Luke describes the appearance of the angel Gabriel to Mary and his announcement of the miraculous birth of Jesus. When Mary questioned such an impossible circumstance, the angel reminded her that "with God nothing shall be impossible" (Luke 1:37).

By being "born of a woman," Christ for all time honored motherhood, and the word "mother" was to become one of the sweetest notes on human tongue. Why did Titian, the Italian artist, when sketching the Madonna give her an Italian face? Why did Rubens give his Madonna a German face? Why did Reynolds in his Madonna favor the English? Undoubtedly because each believed that his own mother was the best type of Mary, the mother of Christ.

Human Development (Luke 2:40-42, 52)

From the human standpoint, Jesus grew in the same manner as other children. He subjected Himself to the laws that govern physical and intellectual development. However, He was always conscious of His deity. Although His sinless nature influenced His growth, it is clear that He received training along the lines of ordinary human progress — instruction, study, thought. In this great condescension, He greatly honored childhood. He who was omnipotent once had a child's beaming eye, a child's light limbs, and a child's soft hair. The greatest gift God ever gave to this world was once a little child. He was of such value that heaven took notice and angels, breaking through the clouds, came down to look at him.

Human Characteristics

The Appearance of a Man (Matt. 14:24-27; Luke 24:36-43; John 4:9; 20:15, 19, 20; Phil. 2:8)

Paul said Christ "was made in the likeness of men" (Phil. 2:7), and we find that to His friends and relatives He appeared as a man. The woman of Samaria designated Him as a Jew by His features and language (John 4:9). Even when He appeared as an apparition in the darkness of the night, walking on the stormy sea, He relieved the fears of the terrified disciples by speaking to them and then joining them in the boat (Matt. 14:24-27, 32).

We possess no photograph of Him, but the four Gospels do not lead us to believe that He was different in appearance from ordinary men. Only at the time of His transfiguration do they point out that "the fashion of his countenance was altered" (Luke 9:29). After the resurrection Jesus seems still to have retained the form of a man. Mary at the tomb mistook Him for the gardener (John 20:15). The two disciples on the way to Emmaus thought He was a traveler, "a stranger in Jerusalem" (Luke 24:18). Even when He miraculously appeared in the upper room behind barred doors the disciples were given evidence of His humanity by His eating in their presence, and of His being the crucified Jesus by the exhibition of His wounds (Luke 24:36-43; John 20:19, 20).

The Garment of Flesh (John 1:14; Heb. 2:14, 16; 10:5)

The New Testament bears clear testimony to the genuine humanity of Christ. The Apostle John declared that "The Word was made flesh and dwelt among us." He further warned against denial of the incarnation (I John 4:2, 3). The writer to the Hebrews likewise stressed the fact of the incarnation when he stated that the Son of God "took not on him the nature of angels; but he took on him the seed of Abraham" (Heb. 2:16). The object of God's redemptive plan was fallen man, not fallen angels. Therefore, God's Son became man in order that He might die in man's place bearing the just penalty for man's sin (II Cor. 5:21). Because He became man, He could die as man's substitute; because He is God the Son, His work on the cross has eternal value. Further, through the incarnation of the Son of God and His death on the cross, Satan's power over man was broken (Heb. 2:14, 15).

Human Limitations

It is important that we think correctly concerning the person of the Incarnate Son of God. He is at once God and Man. He was no less God because of His assumption of humanity; and the genuineness of His humanity was not affected by His deity. Any limitations which Scripture speaks of were self-imposed and were the result of His will to operate on those occasions in the sphere of His humanity. Also, it should be noted that such human limitations ceased after the resurrection. His glorified humanity is not subject to hunger, thirst, weariness, pain, or death.

Physical

Scripture indicates that our Lord subjected Himself to the limitations and needs of the human body, even though He could have exercised His power to overcome those limitations and provide for those needs.

He hungered (Matt. 4:2; 21:18). Although He provided food for the multitudes, He experienced the same need for food.

He thirsted (John 4:7). He needed to quench His thirst with the water of this world, even though He possessed and offered to men the water of life.

He was weary and slept (Matt. 8:24; John 4:6).

He experienced pain and death (I Cor. 15:3; I Pet. 4:1).

Mental (Mark 13:32; Luke 2:52)

Because our Lord was both God and Man, He possessed seemingly contradictory attributes. He was both infinite and finite. On occasion He manifested omnipotence, on other occasions he evidenced weakness. In like manner, the Scriptures present Him both as omniscient (Matt. 9:3, 4; John 1:47-49; 10:15) and as subject to increasing knowledge, and on certain occasions as lacking knowledge (Mark 11:13; 13:32; Luke 2:52). Obviously, Christ purposefully limited Himself on these occasions for reasons known only to Himself.

Human Recognition

The Lord Jesus Christ was universally recognized as a man. Note that He was spoken of as:

Jesus of Nazareth (Luke 18:37; 24:19; John 18:5)

As He had spent all His life, except the last three years, in the town of Nazareth, He was identified with that place. In fact, so few were aware that He was born in Bethlehem that His enemies used the accepted belief of His coming from Galilee as an argument against His being the Messiah. Prophecy had declared that Christ should come "out of the town of Bethlehem, where David was," but so prevailing was the belief that He was a native of Nazareth that even the faith of the scholarly Nicodemus was confronted by this apparent fact (John 7:40-52).

The Son of Joseph (Luke 3:23; John 6:42)

The filial obedience and close attachment of our Lord to Joseph and Mary led everyone to suppose that He was "the carpenter's son." Even the younger half brothers and sisters who were brought up with Jesus in the family at Nazareth refused to accept Him as the Messiah during His earthly ministry. While in the beginning they were doubtless perplexed, later they came to regard him as a fanatic and dreamer (Mark 3:21; John 7:3-5).

The Son of Man (Matt. 26:63, 64; John 1:49-51)

No less than eighty times in the Gospels does Jesus call Himself the *Son of Man*. He seems to have preferred this designation to all others, for even when acquiescing to the recognition that He was the Son of God, He sometimes immediately afterward substituted the title, Son of Man. While we recognize the fact that there is something official in the title, Son of Man — something connected with His relationship to the kingdom of God — nevertheless, our Lord's persistent use of this term makes it evident that He most earnestly desired to identify Himself with the sons of men.

REVIEW QUESTIONS

1. What is Christ's testimony as to His preexistence?
2. Name four New Testament writers that spoke of Christ's preexistence.
3. In what respect was David a prophetic witness of the council of eternity?
4. What Scripture passages teach the eternal existence of Christ?
5. How do we know that Christ was the object worshiped by the angels, and that he shared the glory of God?
6. In what respect was Christ the Creator and the Controller of the universe?
7. What is meant by the incarnation of Christ?
8. What was the purpose of the genealogies in Matthew and Luke?
9. What were some of the human characteristics of our Lord?
10. Give four illustrations of the physical limitations of our Lord.
11. How does Christ's perfect humanity and deity affect our redemption?
12. How does Jesus' use of the title, "Son of Man," show His interest in men?

APPLYING DOCTRINE TO LIFE

1. How does Christ's incarnation help you relate to Him?
2. In what ways would you recognize Christ if He were to appear as a man in your church?

THE DEITY OF CHRIST

7

It is reported that when Marshal Ney entered the presence of Napoleon after directing that masterful retreat from Moscow, the emperor caught him in his arms exclaiming, "The bravest of the brave." But Napoleon was wrong. The bravest of the brave was that humble Galilean who stood calmly before the Jewish council and signed His death warrant by acknowledging that He was the Son of God. The Jewish Sanhedrin condemned Christ to death because they believed Him to be a blasphemer and an impostor. He was crucified because He claimed to be the *Son of God*, thereby asserting His deity. "We have a law," the Jews said to Pilate, "and by our law he ought to die because he made himself the Son of God" (John 19:7).

Jesus might have saved His life if He had not *insisted* that He was the Son of God. But He refused to deny the truth, which meant suffering and the shame of a criminal's crucifixion. His was the greatest of all confessions. A year earlier Peter had made a good confession, but now he was outside denying his Lord because his life was endangered. Had Peter been asked for counsel he no doubt would have advised Jesus to *conceal His real identity* that fatal night. But Jesus refused to compromise. He confessed that He was the Son of God, and did not flinch when put to the crucial test. He was truly the hero of heroes.

Jesus was put to death as an impostor and blasphemer because He claimed to be the Son of God. What evidence is there to support this claim, which was most presumptuous if it were not true? The Gospel writers make it plain.

JESUS, A SUPERNATURAL PERSON

His Virgin Birth (Matt. 1:22, 23; Luke 1:34, 35)

We must not lose sight of the fact that there was something supernatural surrounding the birth of Christ. He was predicted the "seed of the woman," not of the man (Gen. 3:15; Luke 1:34). No laws of heredity are sufficient to account for this generation. This was so exceptional and so significant that seven hundred years before, the prophet Isaiah declared that the sign of the Messiah would be His virgin birth (Isa. 7:14). The fact that the virgin birth is attested by the Scriptures, by tradition, by creeds, and that it is in perfect harmony with all the other facts of Christ's wonderful life, should be sufficient evidence of its truth.

His Marvelous Knowledge (John 2:24, 25; 4:16-19; 7:45, 46; 16:30)

We have already seen that the poverty of Jesus' parents prevented their affording Him more than a common education. Yet He knew more than the wisest and most scholarly men of His day. When the chief priests sent officers to arrest Him, they were so amazed at His wisdom that they hesitated to take Him into custody. When asked by the Pharisees why they returned without Him, they declared, "Never man spoke like this man" (John 7:45, 46). The woman of Samaria was so impressed by His knowledge of her home life that she told her friends, "Come, see a man, which told me all things that ever I did: is not this the Christ?" (John 4:29). His disciples, who had come to know Him better than anyone else, declared the last night He was with them, "Now are we sure that thou knowest all things" (John 16:30).

His Marvelous Power

Jesus pointed to His miracles as evidence that He was a supernatural person. He said, "The works that I do in my Father's name, they bear witness of me. . . . If I do not the works of my Father, believe me not. But if I do, though ye believe not me, believe the works" (John 10:25, 37, 38). There are no less than thirty-six miracles recorded. How many more there may have been we do not know, but these are sufficient to establish His marvelous power.

Power Over Disease (Luke 4:39)

He healed the sick, including the dread and incurable malady of leprosy. He caused the deaf to hear, the dumb to speak, and the blind to see.

Power Over Nature (Matt. 8:26, 27; 14:25; Luke 24:51)

The winds and the waves obeyed His voice, and He defied the power of gravitation by walking on the water, and at the last, ascended into the clouds.

Power Over Demons (Mark 5:8-13; Luke 4:31-36)

Even the spirit world was in subjection to His word. Out of one unfortunate creature a legion of demons were cast and these upon entering the two thousand swine rushed them to their destruction in the sea.

Power Over Death (Mark 5:35, 41, 42; Luke 7:12-15; John 11:32, 43, 44)

Three instances of Jesus' raising the dead are recorded: The daughter of Jairus, who had been dead but a few hours; the son of the widow of Nain, as the funeral procession was bearing his coffin to the grave; the beloved Lazarus, who had been buried four days and was restored to life.

His Own Death and Resurrection (John 10:18)

When asked for a sign to prove that He was the Son of God, Jesus cited the experience of Jonah as an illustration of His impending death and resurrection (Matt. 12:38-40). That He could predict His resurrection and then carry it to fulfillment was truly the greatest manifestation of power over death and the grave that has ever been witnessed by humanity.

His Astonishing Authority (Matt. 7:29)

Again and again it is recorded that the people marveled because Christ spoke "as one having authority and not as the scribes." Where did He get this authority, and how did it differ from the scribes?

There are four sources of authority:

Authority of testimony — facts experienced.

Authority of opinion — scholarship.

Authority of position — recognition.

Authority of inspiration — intuition.

Sometimes when facts and experiences are not obtainable as direct evidence, the opinion of a specialist is recognized as circumstantial evidence. The truth or falsity of this evidence will depend upon the character of the one who gives the testimony. The authority of circumstantial evidence also may be given weight by the position which the witness holds, thus giving him special recognition. He may be a public official or a member of the faculty of a well-known school. The authority of the scribes for the most part was dependent upon their scholarship which made them specialists in the law. They were also recognized because they were members of the Sanhedrin or held other high offices.

The authority of Christ did not depend upon their opinion or position. He had received no recognition for completing a prescribed course of study. He had never been elected to office. His authority, therefore, was dependent upon the testimony of the inerrant Word of God and the Holy Spirit who inspired the Word. This gave more weight to His utterances than the authority of the scholar, or the prestige of a member of the Sanhedrin. This authority was challenged when He assumed the right to forgive sins. The Pharisees justly contended that only God could forgive sins. This Jesus must have been either God or an impostor. His supernatural authority was revealed at:

His Conference With the Doctors (Luke 2:46-49)

Even at the age of twelve, He recognized that He must be about His Father's business. In these first recorded words of Jesus, there is an indication of a consciousness of the unique relationship with His heavenly Father. Note that contrary to Jewish custom, Mary, not Joseph, asked the question "Why hast thou thus dealt with us? Behold thy father and I have sought thee sorrowing." It is remarkable to note that in His reply, Christ makes no allusion to Joseph, and always omits the word "father" when referring to His parents (Matt. 12:48; Mark 3:33, 34). In this incident Christ revealed the fact that it was not Joseph, but God who was His father, and He used this authority in debating with the doctors.

As Revealed at the Transfiguration (Luke 9:30-35)

On the mountain the favorite disciples rejoiced that they had had the privilege of seeing Moses and Elias, those honored characters of the Old Testament. What an opportunity for them now to ask questions and learn from the lips of these translated saints the mysteries of their disappearance! But the voice from heaven was to silence their curiosity by that all-important declaration, "This is my beloved Son: hear ye Him." Eminent men though they were, the voices of Moses and Elias were only those of human authority. Christ alone could speak with supernatural authority.

The Commission of the Twelve (Mark 3:13-19)

When our Lord sent out the Twelve, He demonstrated His deity and His consequent authority when He gave the disciples power over all manner of illness and over demons. Certainly, only God has the ability and authority to dispense such power to men. By this means, Jesus was demonstrating the validity of His claim that He was "the Christ the Son of the Living God" (Matt. 16:16; John 20:31).

JESUS WORSHIPED AS GOD

If Jesus were a man only, why did He permit other men to worship Him? The homage given to Him would be nothing short of sacrilegious idolatry if Christ were not God.

Worshiped After His Birth (Matt. 2:8-11)

Princely scholars from afar, with their homage, and costly gifts were not ashamed to kneel before Him in His humble home. Even King Herod recognized that this was the proper attitude in which to receive Him.

Worshiped by the Leper (Matt. 8:2)

This is the first instance recorded in our Lord's adult ministry of His being worshiped. Why did He not rebuke this act of worship and confess as Peter later did (Acts 10:25, 26), that He was but a man?

Worshiped by the Man Born Blind (John 9:32, 35-38)

It is well to notice this connection that before the grateful beneficiary of Christ's healing power fell at His feet, our Lord revealed Himself to the man as the Son of God.

Worshiped by the Syrophoenician Woman (Mark 7:25-30)

In her conversation with Jesus concerning her demon-possessed daughter, she not only recognized Him as the Messiah by declaring Him the "son of David" (Matt. 15:22), but three times she addressed Him as Lord as she prostrated herself before Him. No wonder our Lord marveled at her faith and honored it by healing her daughter.

Worshiped by the Apostles

There are so many instances recorded of the apostles' worshiping Jesus that we can only name some of them at this time. Most of these instances took place after Peter's notable confession that Jesus was the Son of God (Matt. 16:16). His apostles and some women worshiped Jesus when:

The Storm Was Stilled (Matt. 14:33)

The disciples had witnessed three great miracles within the space of a few minutes. First, they saw the Lord walking upon the water; next, they witnessed the saving of the floundering Peter; third, they observed the boisterous wind had suddenly ceased. In awe and admiration they worshiped Him.

Zebedee's Sons Sought Kingdom Honors (Matt. 20:20)

The mother of Zebedee's children was ambitious. She wanted to see James and John sitting beside the Lord Jesus Christ on the throne of His kingdom. Perhaps it was the audacity of this request and the intense desire to have it granted that caused all three to worship Him. In this request they admitted the truth of His coming kingdom and by His act recognized His kingship.

The Women Recognized Their Risen Lord (Matt. 28:5, 9)

Last at the cross and first at the tomb, these faithful women in their worship not only acknowledged His resurrection but testified to His divinity.

The Risen Christ Appeared on a Mountain (Matt. 28:16, 17)

The risen Lord directed the women to tell the disciples that He would go before them into Galilee, and meet them there in a mountain. When the disciples gathered at the appointed place and beheld their risen Lord, they worshiped Him.

He Finally Ascended to Heaven (Luke 24:51, 52)

The last act of our Lord, as He parted from His disciples, was that of loving benediction, and the last attitude of the disciples, as they saw Him ascending above the clouds, was one of admiration and worship.

JESUS RECOGNIZED AS GOD

There are four different groups or personages that declared that Jesus was God. It has been argued by those who reject Christ as God that in all times people have sought to deify men who have commanded their admiration and affection. Christ's exaltation was not one of man's creation. His was a wider field of recognition than the admiration of a few followers. This acceptance of deity recognized our Lord's prehistoric existence and was not based on elevation attained by human veneration.

The Testimony of Men

John the Baptist (John 1:29, 30)

Not only did the great evangelist bear witness to the prehistoric existence of Christ and the eternal plan to make the God-man the Savior of the world, but our Lord in His debate with the Jews expressly called attention to this testimony to prove His deity (John 5:33-35).

Nathanael (John 1:49)

Before Nathanael became a follower of Jesus, he confessed that the much discussed Teacher was not only the Messiah, but also the Son of God.

Peter (Matt. 16:16)

Peter was the spokesman for the Twelve, and in this great public confession he declared the belief of the other disciples.

Thomas (John 20:28)

How quick Thomas was to worship Jesus when he recognized that the crucified Man was the living God!

The Roman Centurion (Mark 15:39)

Even the official executioner of Jesus substantiated the testimony of friends that the man suffering the death of a criminal was truly the Son of God.

The Testimony of Angels (Luke 2:10, 11)

The message of the angels heard by the shepherds on the night of Jesus' birth proclaimed His deity. The angel that appeared to Mary and later to Joseph also recognized Him as God.

The Testimony of Demons (Matt. 4:3; Luke 4:41)

Satan himself on three occasions admitted Jesus to be the Son of God as he vainly tempted Him to use powers and assume prerogatives that rightfully belong to Him.

The poor demon-possessed people cried out that Jesus was the Son of God, for the demons in them knew that He was Christ (Luke 4:34, 41) but while their testimony was admitted as true, it was not encouraged by our Lord, for He wished that men should make this discovery for themselves.

The Testimony of God

Three times the voice of God was heard from heaven during our Lord's ministry, and on each occasion it was to confirm the fact that Jesus was the Son of God. God's voice was heard at:

Jesus' baptism (Matt. 3:13-17; Luke 3:22)

His transfiguration (Matt. 17:5; Luke 9:35)

The last Passover (John 12:27, 28).

Both John and Peter call attention to the great significance of the transfiguration, not only because of the spoken acknowledgment of Christ's deity, but because of the heavenly honor and glory that were accorded Him on that occasion (John 1:14; II Pet. 1: 16-18). Of the high value of this testimony John writes further, "If we receive the witness of men, the witness of God is greater: for this is the witness of God which he hath testified of his Son" (I John 5:9).

JESUS CLAIMED TO BE GOD

If Jesus was not God He was nothing less than an impostor, for He distinctly declared again and again that He was God. Let us examine His testimony before three distinct groups.

Before His Apostles (John 14:7-11)

Jesus was constantly speaking of His heavenly Father in His conversations with the apostles as well as in His controversies with the Jews. In His farewell address He urged His apostles to accept His statements concerning His relation to the Father, or at least to accept Him on the basis of His miracles. "Believe me that I am in the Father, and the Father in me: or else believe me for the very works' sake" (John 14:11).

Before the Jews (John 10:22-25, 30-33)

At the Feast of Dedication the Jews asked of Jesus the pointed question, "How long dost thou make us to doubt? If thou be the Christ, tell us plainly." Jesus again called attention to His statements to this effect, as well as to the miracles which were offered to substantiate His claims. "I told you, and ye believed not: the works that I do in my Father's name, they bear witness of me." A few minutes later He said, "I and my Father are one." What did the Jews understand Him to mean by such a remark? There was no question in their minds, for they picked up stones to hurl at Him for blasphemy, or as they themselves admitted, "Because that thou, being a man, makest thyself God."

Before the Council (Luke 22:66-71)

We have already seen that this hero of heroes refused the opportunity to clear Himself and go free by speaking a falsehood. When He persisted that He was the Son of God, the Jews declared that He had indicted Himself by His own confession and was therefore worthy of death. This testimony before the high priest was the culmination of all His repeated claims to be nothing less than God.

REVIEW QUESTIONS

1. What testimony of our Lord before the Jewish Sanhedrin led to His condemnation?
2. Name three facts that proclaim Christ a supernatural person.
3. In what five ways was His marvelous power manifested?

4. How did the authority of our Lord differ from that of the scribes and Pharisees?
5. How was the authority of Christ revealed at the transfiguration?
6. Give five incidents in which Jesus was worshiped as God.
7. On what three occasions was our Lord worshiped after His resurrection?
8. What five individuals testified that Jesus was God?
9. What superhuman beings also acknowledged Christ as God?
10. What were the three occasions on which God spoke from heaven and for what purpose?
11. Name three incidents when Christ claimed to be God.
12. Why must we conclude that Jesus is God?

APPLYING DOCTRINE TO LIFE

1. What can you as a teacher do to prepare believers to meet the attacks of false cults who deny the deity of Christ?
2. What benefits accrue to the believer as the result of the deity of Christ?

THE SACRIFICIAL DEATH OF CHRIST

Jesus Christ crucified is a foundational and fundamental doctrine of the Christian Church. The cross is the insignia of our faith. Other great men have been valued for their lives. Christ's greatest blessing to men came through His death.

The cross pervades all Scripture. The Mosaic instructions foreshadow its meaning. The historical books prove its necessity. The Psalms picture its reality. The prophets describe its coming. The Gospels announce its presence. The Acts proclaim its power. The Epistles explain its purpose. Revelation sees the consummation of its blessings.

It is often said, "Cut the Bible anywhere and it bleeds; it is red with redemption truth." One out of every 44 verses in the New Testament deals with the sacrificial death of Christ. It is mentioned in all, 175 times.

While the incarnation divides time, the cross divides eternity. Christ was foreordained as the Lamb slain before the foundation of the world (I Pet. 1:19, 20), and as the Lamb once slain, He will be the theme of endless praise (Rev. 5:13).

It was unreasonable to expect that crucifixion would be employed for the execution of the Messiah. Stoning was the common method of capital punishment among the Jews (Lev. 20:2; Deut. 13:6-10; 17:2-5), and there are illustrations of its use in the Old Testament (Lev. 24:11-14; Num. 15:32-36; I Kings 12:18; 21:13; II Chron. 24:20, 21). Stoning was especially stipulated in the Mosaic law as punishment for idolatry and blasphemy. The Jews requested that our Lord give them permission to stone the sinful woman (John 8:4, 5), and on another occasion they took up stones to hurl at Him when He declared that He was equal with God (John 10:30-33).

Crucifixion was unknown to the Jews when the earliest prophecies of our Lord's death were recorded. The Romans, who introduced this barbarous method of capital punishment, were then hardly in existence. But by a circumstance of events which made the Latins the rulers of the world, the Jews in Christ's time, with other conquered nations, were paying tribute to Caesar. As a province of Rome the right of such a dependent nation to execute its criminals was no longer permitted. Hence the Jews were required to secure the aid of the Roman governor before their prisoners could be put to death. By these strange and unexpected circumstances our Lord was led out to be crucified by the Romans, rather than stoned by the Jews.

Christ said "greater love hath no man than this, that a man lay down his life for his friends" (John 15:13). "But God commendeth his love toward us, in that, while we were yet *sinners*, Christ died for us" (Rom. 5:8). Men have given their lives for their friends, but think of Christ's amazing love for His *enemies*. He came down from the heights of heaven to the lowly cross and bowed His sacred head in shameful, agonizing death. His was the great sacrifice for mankind. God gave His dearly beloved Son for this great sacrifice that "whosoever believeth in him should not perish but have everlasting life" (John 3:16).

PROMINENCE OF THE SACRIFICE

Purpose of the Incarnation

Why was Christ born? The name which Joseph was commanded to give Him indicated He was to be the Savior of His people (Matt. 1:21). He Himself declared that He had come to give His life a ransom for many (Matt. 20:28). From the beginning of His ministry Christ realized that the cross would terminate His life.

Mystery to the Old Testament Prophets

One of the great proofs of the verbal inspiration of the Bible is that the writers did not always understand the message God gave them to record. It appears that the death of Christ, which was predicted centuries before He appeared, was a great mystery to the prophets (I Pet. 1:10-12). Even the angels were not fully advised as to the plan and purpose of the world's greatest tragedy, but it was of such significance that they desired further information about it.

Mystery to the Disciples

There is no better proof that the Bible is the Word of God than the sacrifice of our Lord on Calvary which was clearly described by psalmist and prophets centuries before it took place. Our Lord particularly calls attention to this fact (Luke 24:44). The marvel of the mystery is that the disciples failed to understand the passages in the Old Testament which predicted the history of Jesus Christ and described with wonderful literalness His sufferings and glory. These passages are remarkable in view of the fact that the Jews did not expect their long looked-for Messiah to be put to death, but rather that He would reign as king. Even the disciples could not comprehend the many references our Lord made to His death. The truth of the matter is that the Old Testament has much to say about a coming king and prophesies about a crucified Savior. The angel that announced to Mary the birth of Jesus said nothing about His premature death, but instead predicted that "He shall be great, and shall be called the Son of the Highest: and the Lord shall give unto

Him the throne of his father David: And He shall reign over the house of Jacob forever; and of His kingdom there shall be no end" (Luke 1:32, 33). No wonder Mary pondered these things in her heart and that a sword pierced her own perplexed soul as she stood at the cross and beheld the suffering of her uncrowned Son.

Place in the Gospels

A study of the Gospels impresses one with the silence concerning the many years, and the stress upon the last week of our Lord's life. If, as some contend, the life rather than the death of Christ is the important subject, is it not strange that each of the Gospel writers gave the briefest accounts of the events in Jesus' life, but described in detail the events connected with His death? That the atonement was the all-important purpose of Christ's coming is proved by the fact that John, having related incidents and conversations others omitted, joined with Matthew, Mark, and Luke in making much of our Lord's last week at Jerusalem. Of the 21 chapters in John, 10 describe the events leading up to the crucifixion and resurrection.

Paul made the cross the theme of his first and many other sermons (I Cor. 15:1-3). Like Peter at Pentecost, Paul particularly pointed out that Christ's death was "according to the scriptures."

PROPHECY CONCERNING THE SACRIFICE

More than one-third of the Old Testament is prophecy, with Christ its central theme. Note the relationship of the Old Testament to the last book of the New Testament: In the one the Savior and King is prophesied; in the other, the Savior and King is glorified. The work of the Savior was predicted in three ways:

By Symbol

When Paul said that "the law was our schoolmaster to bring us unto Christ" (Gal. 3:24), he included the ceremonial law. The shedding of blood by the offering of animal sacrifices for the redemption of sin was a symbol of the great Sacrifice (Lev. 1:2, 11, 15; 8:15), and a constant emphasis on the all-important truth that "without shedding of blood is no remission" of sin (Heb. 9:11-14, 19-22). The office of the high priest was instituted that there might be a representative of the people to offer up sacrifices. As the great High Priest, our Lord offered Himself as the all-sufficient sacrifice for sin.

By Type

There are said to be 333 striking Old Testament pictures of Christ's sacrificial death. In the beginning of human history only sacrifices requiring the shedding of blood met with God's approval. Cain's offering did not typify the sacrifice of life and was not acceptable (Heb. 9:22; 11:4). Let us consider two outstanding types:

The Passover Lamb

The lamb required for the celebration of the Passover (Exod. 12:5-7, 13) was an appropriate type of the great Sacrifice, typifying the sinless Lamb of God whose blood was to save from eternal death. In the substitution of the Lord's Supper for the Passover, Christ became the Paschal Lamb.

The Brazen Serpent

The fiery serpents that invaded the camp of Israel represented sin and its fatal consequences. The brazen serpent erected by Moses (Num. 21:9) represented the Sin-Bearer who was "made sin for us" in order to remove the penalty of sin. Christ indicated that it was a picture of the crucifixion — the uplifted cross (John 3:14, 15).

By Word

Just what experiences our Lord passed through we learn not so much from the Gospel narrators, who wrote what they saw and heard, but from the prophets who recorded the story by divine inspiration, centuries before it took place. Prophecy provides another Gospel that is corroborative and supplementary to Matthew, Mark, Luke, and John. In the New Testament we see only glimpses of the terrible conflicts of our Lord on the cross; in the Old Testament we see all His anguish. In the Gospels we have what Christ said and did, and what was said and done to Him; in prophecy we see His inner life — what He thought, and how He felt, and how He lived in the presence of His God and Father.

The Savior Pierced (Ps. 22:16; Zech. 12:10; Luke 24:40; John 19:34)

What a picture is given us of the mob closing in at the foot of the cross. They were on all sides, like the packs of dogs in Palestine that were wont to surround their prey. There He was in the center with hands and feet pierced. Yet those scarred hands were to be evidence to the disciples that the risen Lord was the very man who had passed through this terrible ordeal. And there shall come a time when the Jews, who have long rejected Jesus Christ as their Messiah, shall recognize Him as the same one they had pierced. When they recognize the awful mistake of the centuries, "they shall mourn for him, as one mourneth for his only son . . . In that day shall there be a great mourning in Jerusalem" (Zech. 12: 10, 11).

The Savior Thirsting (Ps. 22:14, 15; 69:21; Matt. 27:34, 48; John 19:28, 29)

Note the words of John, "Jesus knowing that all things were now accomplished, that the scripture might be fulfilled, saith, I thirst" (John 19:28). He did not give vent to His own suffering until He knew all that He had come to do for man's salvation had been accomplished. And here is recorded both in prophecy and history the one kindness shown to our suffering Lord as He hung on the cross. When He cried of His thirst, someone offered Him an opiate that would have lessened the physical pain. But we note that He refused the vinegar which was mingled with gall. He bore the full penalty of our sins in every respect.

The Savior Stripped (Ps. 22:17, 18; 34:20; Luke 23:34; John 19:23, 24, 32-37)

Seated in front of the cross, the Roman soldiers, the lowest strata of Roman citizenry, the men whose lives were characterized by violence and sin, gambled for His clothing. Though these men cared not for God, or His Word, or the dying Son of God upon the cross, they fulfilled that Word that day, for the prophet had declared, "They parted my garments among them, and cast lots upon my vesture."

And yet the same unseen power that caused the soldiers to gamble over the Savior's garments, later withheld the hammer blows that would have broken His limbs. Not only had the prophet declared that not a bone of Him should be broken, but centuries before when Israel fled from Egypt, not a bone of the paschal lamb was broken. When the Lamb that was slain from the foundation of the world became Israel's Passover, it was fitting that He should be offered up in the same manner. Here again we see the marvel of God's providence, for if our Lord had been stoned to death or had even suffered bodily injury from one of the boulders with which the Jews had threatened Him, He would no longer have been the perfect Lamb for the Passover sacrifice. Thus in the substitution of crucifixion for stoning, Christ in His death became a perfect antitype of the paschal lamb.

The Savior Humiliated (Isa. 53:12; Mark 15:27,28; Luke 22:37; 23:34a)

In Isaiah 53 there are at least ten predictions regarding the humiliation of the King of glory. The crowning insult was numbering Him with the transgressors. What it meant to the absolutely holy Son of God to be crucified between thieves we cannot fathom. It was the outrage of the ages. It was an indignity that this world had never seen before and never will again. But in the midst of His humiliation He became a Savior of the transgressors with whom He was numbered.

PROVISION OF THE SACRIFICE

The Lamb Provided for Abraham

A bearded partiarch rose early one morning and awakened his son, that they might begin the three day journey to the mount of which God had spoken (Gen. 22:1-13). God had commanded him to slay his only son as a sacrifice on the mountain altar. Finally they arrived at the appointed place. Imagine the anguish of the father's heart when the son broke the silence with his innocent question, "My father . . . behold the fire and the wood: but where is the lamb for a burnt-offering?" How Abraham must have stifled his emotions as he said brokenly, "My son, God will provide Himself a lamb."

The Lamb Provided for the World

Abraham spoke prophetically (John 8:56). The ram substituted for Isaac was a type of the Lamb of God which was to be provided twenty centuries later (John 1:29). Abraham's son was spared in the moment of death. But when God led His only begotten Son to the cross, He could not release Him from death. Can anyone measure the greatness of that love which made the everlasting Father not only place His Son on the altar, but thrust the sacrificial knife into the heart of His only begotten, beloved Son?

PURPOSE OF THE SACRIFICE

Why was Abraham's son spared and God's Son sacrificed? Why was it necessary for our Lord Jesus Christ to suffer a painful and shameful death?

The Fulfillment of Scripture (Luke 24:25, 26; I Cor. 15:3)

Christ's sacrifice was necessary in order to fulfill Scripture. This our Lord declared to the travelers on the road to Emmaus. This Paul wrote to the Corinthians. God's Word cannot be broken; therefore, "the Lamb slain from the foundation of the world" was in due time revealed that the unchangeable decree might be executed.

The Holiness of God (Ps. 47:8; 24:3, 4; Isa. 6:3)

In a former lesson we have seen the perfection of God's holiness. To God sin of every character is awful, blackening, degrading. His whole nature turns in utter abhorrence against it. The Scriptures plainly teach that death has been the penalty of sinful creatures who have dared to venture into His holy presence. A righteous God could not possibly ignore sin. To do so would have been contrary to His own holiness and would have resulted in moral chaos in the world.

The Sinfulness of Man (Rom. 3:10-20; Gal. 3:13, 14)

All men have sinned. This is the plain teaching of Scripture. There is original sin, in which all men partake of the transgression of their first parents, who not only fell from the holy estate in which they were created, but by disobeying God brought all their descendants into an estate of sin and misery. The sinfulness of man was made evident in the giving of the law. The law God gave did not remove sin, but only made it the more glaring.

In view of the holiness of God and the sinfulness of man, the question naturally arises: How is the mercy of God to be manifested so that His holiness will not be compromised by His assuming a merciful attitude toward sinful men in the granting of forgiveness? If God and the sinner are to be brought together, something must be done to remove sin, for while God loves the sinner, He has and will always continue to have hatred for sin.

PROPITIATION THROUGH SACRIFICE (Rom. 3:25; I John 2:2; 4:10)

Propitiation means satisfaction. The mercy seat covering the ark of the covenant was typical of Christ. The New Testament refers to it as the place of propitiation (Exod. 25:22; Heb. 9:5; same word in Rom. 3:25). The death of Christ for man's sin satisfied the demands of God's holiness and righteousness relative to the sin question and the offending sinner. Therefore, all who come to God through faith on the basis of that gracious cross work receive the forgiveness of sins, the gift of eternal life, and are given a perfect standing in God's sight (justified). It is Christ's death that is the righteous ground on which a righteous God can justify sinners without compromising His holiness and righteousness. It must ever be remembered that "the carnal mind is enmity against God" and "to be carnally minded is death" (Rom. 8:6, 7). God can have no dealings with man until his sin is removed, and only Christ's blood is sufficient for this.

Sufficient for All (Heb. 2:9)

Christ tasted death for every man, and sinners of all sorts, degrees, and conditions may have a share in the benefits of his redemptive work. The Greeks invited only the cultured, the Romans called the strong, and the Jews believed only the religious were entitled to salvation. Christ bids all to come. "Whosoever will, let him take the water of life freely" (Rev. 22:17). No one can deny the *whosoever* of the gospel. The invitation to partake of the blessings of Christ's death is universal.

Efficacious to the Believer

A sovereign God who offers a gracious pardon to an undeserving sinner has a right to lay down conditions for the reception of these benefits. There must be an acceptance of God's gift. Salvation made possible by Christ's sacrificial death is unlimited, but only those who believe and accept it can be saved. Only man's unbelief limits the atonement (John 3:16-18; 5:40).

THE POWER OF THE SACRIFICE

It is almost impossible to measure the far-reaching results of the atonement. Every blessing, material or spiritual, that has come to man in the history of the world, has been brought about by the death of Christ. Without it God could not have given blessings, for because of his sin man had forfeited every claim to God's benevolence. It will take eternity to appreciate all that the great sacrifice means. Observe its power over sin:

Saves From the Penalty of Sin (Rom. 3:24; 5:1; 8:1; Titus 2:14)

Christ died in our place on Calvary, suffering the just penalty due our sin, in order that we might be delivered from the guilt, defilement, and penalty of sin through faith in Him.

Secures From the Power of Sin (Rom. 6:6-18; 8:12)

While Satan cannot change the destiny of the believer, he still is able to tempt him with sin. But "there is power in the blood" of Jesus Christ to give every Christian victory over temptation (Heb. 2:18). Sin no longer need have dominion over him (Rom. 6:12-18).

Separates From the Presence of Sin (Rev. 21:27)

The believer in Christ can look forward to the certainty of an entrance into that holy and happy habitation where no evil can gain entrance. This unmerited, indescribable place has been provided only by the death of Jesus Christ.

REVIEW QUESTIONS

1. In what respects is the crucifixion of Christ the foundation and fundamental doctrine of Christianity?
2. What was the Jewish method of execution and why was it not employed in the death of our Lord?
3. Of what significance is it that the crucifixion was a mystery to the Old Testament prophets as well as to the disciples?
4. How large a place does the sacrificial death of Christ have in the Gospels?
5. Give two Old Testament types of the crucifixion.
6. Name four Old Testament predictions of His ignominious death.
7. How was the lamb, which was provided for Abraham, a prophetic type of the crucifixion?
8. What three things suggest the purpose of the sacrifice?
9. What Scripture passages declare the sinfulness of man?
10. What is meant by propitiation?
11. If propitiation is sufficient for all, why will not all men be saved?
12. What three far-reaching benefits are secured for the believer through the sacrifice of Christ?

APPLYING DOCTRINE TO LIFE

1. What does the death of Christ mean to you?
2. How should the fact of Christ's death affect your relationships with others?

THE RESURRECTION OF CHRIST

9

The resurrection of the Lord Jesus Christ is an historic fact and, as such, it has been substantiated by many infallible proofs. All English-speaking people believe that eighty years before the birth of Christ, Julius Caesar, with two Roman legions, landed in Britain on the coast of Kent. No one thinks of doubting that. If eternal salvation depended on believing that fact, every student of history would accept it. Yet the actual historic proof of this is far less complete, cogent, and convincing, than is the evidence that Christ died and rose again. All Americans believe that there is such a thing as the Declaration of Independence. Why? Because George Washington, Thomas Jefferson, and their contemporaries so stated. Since 1776 Americans have celebrated the Fourth of July as a memorial of national independence. But while the resurrection of Jesus Christ occurred centuries before the signing of the declaration of American independence, Easter is more widely observed today than the Fourth of July. More significant in our study is the fact that there was not one word of prophecy recorded concerning either the conquest of Britain by Julius Caesar or the gaining of American independence. The foretelling of the resurrection of Jesus Christ, together with the many other infallible proofs, such as the testimony of eye-witnesses and the remarkable attending circumstances, makes it the best attested fact in history.

THE EVIDENCE OF FULFILLED PROPHECY
Old Testament Predictions

Nothing in prophecy occupies more attention than the death and resurrection of Christ. At least twenty-five Old Testament prophecies were fulfilled in one day.

Specific Predictions (Ps. 16:10; Isa. 53:9)

Isaiah had a vision of our Lord's burial. Though He died with the wicked and according to the usual proceedings would have been buried with them in the place where He was crucified, the prophet declared strangely enough that the Lord Jesus Christ should be honored with an exquisite funeral. Although the betrayal money, which the conscience-stricken Judas returned to the chief priests, was used to purchase the potter's field for the burial of the friendless (Matt. 27:3-8), the body of our Lord was not permitted such ignominious disposal. The wealthy Joseph of Arimathaea begged the body of Jesus from Pilate, and gave it the attention befitting a man of great renown and distinction. No expense was spared in the provision and preparation of the royal sepulchre. In having the body placed "in his new tomb," this wealthy and influential disciple of our Lord bestowed upon it as much care as would have been given his own son (Matt. 27:57-60).

Long before Isaiah saw in vision the Savior dying with the wicked and yet buried with the wealthy, David spoke expressly about His resurrection: "For thou wilt not leave my soul in hell; neither wilt thou suffer thine Holy One to see corruption" (Ps. 16: 10). Our Lord would go into Sheol (hell or the grave), but for a brief time only. His body would sink into the outer prison of the grave, but not to corruption. Death and hell would not be able to hold Him. In other words, Jesus Christ would be entombed long enough for conclusive evidence of His death, but not long enough for His body "to see corruption." The repeated mention of "the third day" in this connection is most significant. It will be remembered that Lazarus, whom Jesus raised, had been in the grave four days and that decomposition of the body had already begun (John 11:39). Our Lord, however, was released from the tomb on the third day, before there were any signs of disintegration. Could one ask for anything more definite and more clearly defined than this?

Types of Personal Experience (Matt. 12:40; Heb. 11:17-19)

The experience of Isaac was not only typical of the atonement, but also of the resurrection of Jesus Christ. From the moment that Abraham began to obey God's command to offer up his only son as a sacrifice, Isaac was a dead man. The father was fully resolved to follow out the divine instructions, believing "that God was able to raise him up, even from the dead; from whence also he received him in a figure." It was "on the third day" (Gen. 22:4) that God interrupted Abraham in the midst of the sacrifice, providing the substitutionary lamb and restoring the doomed son to the father's embrace.

The experience of Jonah was even more typical of our Lord's resurrection. When the scribes and Pharisees clamored for a sign or special miracle to prove that He was the Messiah, Jesus declared that "as Jonas was three days and three nights in the whale's belly; so shall the Son of man be three days and three nights in the heart of the earth." Christ, the most intelligent of teachers, observed the law of apperception by teaching the unknown in terms of the known. It is inconceivable that He would have used a recognized myth to convince unbelieving Jews of His own burial and resurrection. Nothing is more conclusive from the reading of the Gospels than that both the disciples and the Jews accepted the experience of Jonah as fact, but were loath to believe in the coming resurrection of Christ.

New Testament Predictions

All of the New Testament predictions regarding His resurrection were spoken by our Lord. The first was uttered at the very beginning of His ministry, and the last on the final journey to Jerusalem but a few weeks before the crucifixion.

Christ's First Prophecy (John 2:18-22)

On the occasion of the Jewish Passover our Lord indignantly drove out the desecrators of the temple who were using its sacred portals to sell their merchandise to the assembled multitudes. When the Jews challenged Him for a sign to show that He had authority for such action, Christ declared His power to rise from the dead: "Destroy this temple, and in three days I will raise it up." No one understood what He meant by these words, but after His resurrection the disciples recalled the incident and then realized that "he spake of the temple of his body." It is not to be wondered that they did not understand this hidden prophecy when they failed to grasp the plain predictions He made later.

Christ's Second Prophecy (Matt. 16:21; Mark 8:31; Luke 9:22)

More than a year passed before the second prediction of the resurrection. This occurred at the height of our Lord's popularity, shortly after He had fed the five thousand and the people had attempted to make Him king. We can imagine how shocked the disciples must have been to hear that their popular leader would "suffer many things of the elders and chief priests and scribes, and be killed." It is little wonder that the impetuous Peter protested. So distressed and confused by the dismal thought of His death were they, that the assurance of the Lord's resurrection seems not to have made any impression on the disciples. Yet this prediction was definite, even to the time when the resurrection should take place.

Christ's Third Prophecy (Matt. 17:9; Luke 9:28-31)

After the first discouraging announcement of His death, our Lord inspired three of His disciples by a glimpse of His glory on the Mount of Transfiguration. At that time Moses and Elijah appeared and conversed with the glorified Savior. It is interesting to note that the topic of their discussion was "his decease which he should accomplish at Jerusalem" (Luke 9:31) — the theme that had been so unwelcome to the disciples. This wonderful conference on the mountain top in which the Old Testament prophets joined was not only intended as another prediction of the crucifixion, but also to give Peter, James, and John some conception of the importance of its place in God's program. When they came down from the mountain our Lord again reminded the three disciples that He would rise from the dead, for He charged them not to speak to anyone of what they had seen until after His resurrection (Matt. 17:9).

Christ's Fourth Prophecy (Matt. 17:22, 23; Mark 9:31; Luke 9:43-45)

Despite the association of the crucifixion and resurrection with their wonderful mountain experience, the disciples who had witnessed the transfiguration were still unwilling to accept the announcement. Once more our Lord was obliged to speak explicitly of these coming events. Once more the disciples failed to comprehend it all. We read, "They were exceeding sorry," but while they had begun to realize what Christ meant when He spoke about being put to death, they still did not understand the meaning of His "rising again."

Christ's Fifth Prophecy (Matt. 20:18, 19; Mark 10:34; Luke 18:33)

And now the time drew nigh for the all-important events of the Lord's ministry to take place. He was preparing to attend His last Passover at Jerusalem. Unlike other celebrations of the feast He had observed with His disciples, this fateful one would usher in His death and resurrection. Once more He went over these vital matters with His disciples, but if they grasped His unwelcome instruction at all, it was not very clear in their minds. Scarcely had He spoken of the cross and the empty tomb when the ambitious mother of the sons of Zebedee requested that James and John be accorded the chief places in the coming kingdom (Matt. 20:20, 21). Their minds were filled with thoughts of His throne and the day of His power. They were anxious to share in Christ's reward, but did not realize that they must first be partakers of His sufferings.

THE TESTIMONY OF THE ASTONISHED FRIENDS

The closest friends of Jesus did not expect that He would rise again. They considered their cause ended at the crucifixion.

The Women (Mark 16:1-11; Luke 24:1-11; John 20:11-18)

Study the various accounts of Mary Magdalene. She went to mourn, not to greet her Lord. "Who shall roll us away the stone?" the women asked. They were astonished to find it rolled away and the tomb empty. It was only after our Lord appeared personally to Mary Magdalene, and the angels reminded the other women of His oft-repeated predictions of His resurrection, that they were willing to believe that someone had not come and stolen the body.

The Disciples (Luke 24:13-31; John 20:1-10; John 20:24-28)

When the women, finally convinced, hastened to tell the disciples, "their words seemed to them as idle tales, and they believed them not" (Luke 24:11). It was only when Peter and John came to the empty tomb and saw the discarded grave clothes still retaining the shape of the body that they were convinced a robbery was impossible. On the way to Emmaus, Jesus' companions could not believe that Christ was with them until He broke bread and vanished out of their sight. Even when Christ finally appeared to all of the disciples in the upper room, the doubting Thomas would not believe it was anything but an hallucination. It was only after he was asked to put his fingers in the nail prints and to thrust his hand into Christ's side that he declared, "My Lord and my God."

This detailed evidence of the utter *unbelief* of the disciples finally destroys the attempted theory that the risen Lord was the creation of excited, nervous, and ardent expectations. The disciples were willing to brand the women's tales as hallucinations, and were far from expecting that they would eventually be convinced of what they could not previously conceive. Peter, who permitted a maid to frighten him on the eve of Calvary, possessed the courage of a lion at Pentecost. Unquestionably something most extraordinary had happened between those two days. The enthusiasm of the disciples which could not be diminished by persecution and martyrdom was not built upon a known falsehood. The resurrection was made the cornerstone of their preaching.

An Eminent Scholar (I Cor. 15:1-9)

There was an eminent scholar at that time who refused to accept the earnest, enthusiastic testimony of the disciples. He branded the resurrection as an out-and-out lie. He went further, and persecuted all who proclaimed it. But one day the attitude of this great intellect was completely changed. The living Christ called down to him from heaven and demanded a reason for his persecuting hatred. This convinced the philosopher of Tarsus that Christ had risen. He saw Christ's glory, he heard Christ's voice, and he then and there devoted his life to the task of bearing testimony to what he saw and heard.

But this new disciple of our Lord did not content himself merely by rehearsing the things which he had seen and heard. His scholarly mind investigated all the evidences of the resurrection of Christ that they might be set down in writing as unanswerable arguments for the years to come. He interviewed Peter and John. He questioned James, the brother of the Lord. He saw the women who were with Jesus. He visited the church of Jerusalem which had been gathered by the risen Christ. He confirmed the report that five hundred had seen Jesus at one time. So convincing were the proofs which he was able to gather that he went into heathen cities and presented them before some of the most intellectual people, and they accepted them. The thousands of converts of the world's greatest missionary could have investigated every statement which Paul made and could, like him, have interviewed the living witnesses of the resurrection of Jesus Christ.

THE EVIDENCE OF CHRIST'S ENEMIES

The Precaution to Insure Christ's Death (John 19:31-37)

By this torturous means of execution, the victim died slowly and sometimes lingered thirty-eight to forty hours before expiring. Josephus, the Jewish historian, tells of the recovery of one of three friends for whom he had a release, after having been on the cross for some time. This circumstance encouraged some people to argue that Christ merely swooned and revived in the cooler recesses of the tomb.

The Jews were unwilling that the three criminals should remain hanging on the cross on the Sabbath day. According to their own law they were obliged to bury criminals the same day that they were executed. For this reason, on the eve of the Sabbath, they besought Pilate to let the soldiers complete the execution. The two thieves were immediately despatched, but believing Jesus to be already dead, the Roman soldiers certified to this fact and thrust a spear into His side. His death, then, was positively proved by His enemies and positively pronounced by unbiased witnesses whose business it was to execute order.

The Precaution to Guard the Sepulchre (Matt. 27:62-66)

The strongest evidence of the risen Lord was the absent body. Where did it go? The disciples did not take it. They could not take it. They had no thought of such action. The Jews did not take it. On the other hand, every precaution was taken to prevent the stealing of His body, for they remembered Christ's saying that He would rise again on the third day. In order that His friends might not circulate such a report, the chief priests and Pharisees requested of Pilate that the sepulchre be sealed and a guard set over it. This was intended positively to prevent any possibilities of tampering with the body by the disciples. But the disciples, as we have seen, had no such intention. When Joseph, the Arimathean, had his servants roll the great stone before the mouth of the tomb, it was like sealing up a lost cause.

The Precaution to Bribe the Authorities (Matt. 28:11-15)

Imagine the predicament of Christ's enemies when the guards told them of the terrible earthquake and the appearance of supernatural creatures who had rolled away the great stone as though it were a swinging door, and for fear of them they were obliged to flee for their lives.

Now there was only one thing which the enemies of Christ could do. They bribed the Roman authorities who were always willing to do anything provided they were paid sufficiently. And so the chief priests and elders having taken counsel advised, "Say ye his disciples came by night, and stole him away while we slept. And if this come to the governor's ears, we will persuade him, and secure you. So they took the money, and did as they were taught." This deception by the religious leaders was designed to explain away the resurrection by making the disciples responsible for the removal of Christ's dead body. In these religious leaders we have a fulfillment of the words of Christ that they would not be persuaded "though one rise from the dead" (Luke 16:31).

THE EVIDENCE OF THE IMPARTIAL WITNESSES (Acts 5:34-40)

The Witness of Gamaliel

So great an impression did the preaching of the resurrection make upon the people of Jerusalem that the great lawyer, Gamaliel, said to the authorities who tried to crush it, ". . . let them alone: for if this counsel or this work be of men, it will come to nought: But if it be of God, ye cannot overthrow it; lest haply ye be found even to fight against God."

But the apostles were not left alone; they were hunted, and persecuted, and slain. Nevertheless, their work came not to nought. Based upon faith in the resurrection, millions of men, women, and children have been loved, sought out, and blessed.

The Witness of the Church

The Christian Church is a great witnessing fact to the resurrection. Where did it get its missionary life? It was received from the risen Christ who said, "Go ye into all the world and preach the gospel to every creature." What gospel does it bring to the world? The gospel of the resurrection: "If thou shalt confess with thy mouth the Lord Jesus, . . . thou shalt be saved" (Rom. 10:9). Upon this creed the great Christian Church has been established.

The Witness of the Lord's Day

How does worship on the first day of the week prove the resurrection? For centuries the Jews had recognized the seventh day as the day of rest and worship. But the resurrection was such an important factor in the life of the church, that Christians began worshiping on the first day of the week to commemorate the resurrection of Christ.

The Witness of the Resurrection

The very observance of Easter in Europe, America, and Australia, and even in Asia and Africa, where millions of people are neither friends nor foes of Christ, is overwhelming evidence of the resurrection. Why does the domestic world, the commercial world, and the social world make so much of this great event, if there be no risen Lord, and no hope of a resurrection body? This year all over the civilized world men are writing 19____. What does this mean? Great men have died, but we do not number the years from their birth or death. How do we explain that we are writing 19__ years after Christ instead of _____ years after George Washington, or _____ years after Julius Caesar, _____ years after Alexander the Great? This was no ordinary man who changed the course of time and gave the world its calendar. Every time a date is written it is a witness to the resurrection! Explanation can be given on no other ground than that corroborated by reliable witnesses that Jesus was the Son of God, and that He arose from the dead as He predicted.

REVIEW QUESTIONS

1. How do we know that the resurrection of Christ is better established as an historic fact than the Declaration of Independence?
2. What specific predictions of the resurrection are found in the Old Testament?
3. In what respects were Isaac and Jonah types of the resurrection?
4. How many prophecies did our Lord make concerning His resurrection? When was the first uttered, and on what occasion the last?
5. What evidence is there that the friends of our Lord did not believe in the resurrection?
6. What finally convinced Peter and John of this fact?
7. What circumstance led Paul to believe in the resurrection?
8. How did the enemies of Christ show some faith in his predictions?
9. What was the witness of Gamaliel to the resurrection?
10. How did the Christian Church get its missionary life from the resurrection?
11. How does the observance of the Lord's Day prove the resurrection?
12. How is the observance of Easter a witness to the resurrection?

APPLYING DOCTRINE TO LIFE

1. What effect does the resurrection of Christ have upon the Christian's present and future experience?
2. What should be a teacher's attitude toward Sunday activities in the light of the resurrection?

THE RETURN AND REIGN OF CHRIST

10

In emphasizing the sacrificial death of the Lord Jesus Christ, many have overlooked the importance of His second coming to reign as King over all the earth. Some have concluded that when Christ was born as the King of the Jews and rejected by His own people, the divine plan for a kingdom was abandoned and the Church substituted. Others make no distinction between the Church and the kingdom. These views are not the teaching of Scripture. Christ is both Savior and King. The Great Sacrifice accomplished, the High Priest is now in heaven. We anticipate His future entrance as King into His kingdom.

The prophets of the Old Testament were perplexed, Peter tells us, because the Holy Spirit revealed unto them both "the sufferings of Christ, and the glory that should follow" (I Pet. 1:10, 11). They could not understand how Messiah could be both Sacrifice and King. They little dreamed that there would be a long interval of time between the crucifixion and the coronation, when the Church — a mystery not revealed to the prophets — would have its day and accomplish its purpose. It was not until the day of transfiguration that the first light illuminated the problem. After our Lord had disclosed to His disciples His coming death, three of them were privileged to catch a glimpse of "the glory that should follow," on the Mount of Transfiguration. This our Lord declared to be a vision of "the Son of man coming into his kingdom" (Matt. 16:28), and Peter later associated it with the "coming of our Lord Jesus Christ" as an event still future (II Pet. 1:16-18).

THE RETURN OF CHRIST

His Coming Assured (Matt. 24:29, 30; Mark 14:62; Luke 17:24, 25; 21:25-27; I Thess. 4:13-18; Heb. 9:28)

There are no less than three hundred references in the New Testament that assure us of the second coming of the Lord Jesus Christ. In addition to His own specific statements, all of the writers in the New Testament refer to it, while the book of Revelation is the "unveiling" of His glorious person. While the terrible tribulation period and other impending events are predicted as sure and certain signs of His coming, the exact day and hour is not revealed. The frequent use of the word "watch" in the New Testament is to teach us that the second coming of the Lord must always be regarded as imminent. Like the motion to adjourn in parliamentary law, it takes precedence over any other event.

His Coming in Person (Zech. 14:4; Acts 1:11; Rev. 1:7)

Forty days after his resurrection, Jesus was talking with an assembled group of His disciples and followers when suddenly, while they beheld, He was taken up into heaven, and a cloud received Him out of their sight. As the disciples stood there staring up in amazement, two angels said to them, "Ye men of Galilee, why stand ye gazing up into heaven? This same Jesus, which is taken up from you into heaven, shall so come *in like manner* as ye have seen him go into heaven" (Acts 1:11).

In the moment of their keenest desolation and loss, this promise was given to the disciples. It also comes to us and to believers of every generation as an assurance that Christ will literally come again. His coming will not be just a spiritual visitation, but a personal return. *From* the earth He ascended, and *to* the earth He will return: "And his feet shall stand in that day upon the Mount of Olives, which is before Jerusalem on the east" (Zech. 14:4). With a real body He left them, and with a real body He will come back; it shall be a resurrected, and glorified body, but we shall recognize Him just as truly as Thomas did when he was shown the nailprints in the Lord's hands.

They saw Him go away into heaven, and every eye shall clearly see Him when He descends from heaven to the earth. "Behold, he cometh with clouds; and every eye shall see him, and they also which pierced him: and all kindreds of the earth shall wail because of him" (Rev. 1:7).

His Coming with His Saints (Jude 14, 15; Rev. 19:14)

When the Son of Man comes in the clouds of heaven with power and great glory, He will not come alone. "Behold, the Lord cometh with ten thousands of his saints" (Jude 14). John saw them and wrote, "And the armies which were in heaven followed him upon white horses, clothed in fine linen, white and clean" (Rev. 19:14). The armies, then, must be the saints; not the Church alone, but the saints of Old Testament times, as well as those slain by the Beast in the great tribulation. All follow in the train of their now triumphant Lord, when He comes to put down Satan and his followers forever, and to reign in righteousness.

The Great Captain will be mounted on a white horse, and the saints likewise will ride forth on horses of all white, for they are all royal and righteous, through Him, and come forth to share in His work of conquering, judging, and ruling. They will wear no armor, for they are immortal, but will be clothed in fine linen, white, and clean, for their garments have been washed in the blood of the Lamb.

Have you ever had that strange conception of the future life of the saved which picture them as reclining idly on a golden street or playing a harp by a crystal stream? We are not saved to eternal idleness nor to the feverish rush of activity such as we know here. But there will be a place for each of us in God's plan for the eternal ages. We cannot look that far ahead now, but from what is revealed, we see that the saints will have an important work to do in that day of the establishing of Christ's kingdom. John here pictures them sharing in the battle and the triumph which bring in the kingdom. Paul tells us that the saved shall share in judging the world (I Cor. 6:2). We also read that the saints shall reign with Him (Rev. 20:6) and His servants shall serve Him (Rev. 22:3).

His Coming in Power and Glory (Matt. 24:29-31; 26:64; Mark 8:38; Luke 21:25-27)

A number of the passages to which we have already referred have spoken of the power and the glory of the second coming of our Lord. Now we turn to still others. Matthew, Mark, and Luke all record Christ's prophecy of His coming back to earth at the end of the days of tribulation, and in this prediction He speaks of His coming with great power and glory.

Again, in that infamous trial to which the Holy Son of God was subjected, when the high priest sought to force Christ to answer whether or not He was the Christ, the Son of God, Jesus said to His accusers, "Hereafter shall ye see the Son of man sitting on the right hand of power, and coming in the clouds of heaven" (Matt. 26: 64). Peter speaks of the transfiguration as a glimpse of "the power and coming of our Lord Jesus Christ" (II Pet. 1:16). All this power and glory will be in sharp contrast to His first appearance here on earth as the Son of Man.

Think what will be the feeling of those who have made light of Christ! Imagine the agony of soul of those who mocked Him in Pilate's hall and helped to hang Him on the tree! John mentions in particular that they which pierced Him shall see Him in the hour of His triumph (Rev. 1:7).

Not only man will tremble in the presence of such great power and glory, but the whole universe will shake. The Mount of Olives will cleave in two, the hills and the mountains will move, the stars will fall from their places, and the sun and moon hide their faces.

His Coming in Judgment (Ps. 2; Zeph. 1:14-18; Matt. 16:27; II Thess. 1:7-10; Jude 15)

Why will the nations wail at the sign of His appearing? Why will God laugh while "the heathen rage, . . . the kings of the earth set themselves, and the rulers take counsel together, against the Lord, and against his anointed"? Because He comes in power and great glory to judge the world. He will break the rebellious "with a rod of iron," and "dash" the ungodly "in pieces like a potter's vessel," as the psalmist expresses it in that prophetic psalm of the Messiah's return to establish His kingdom.

Read Zephaniah's graphic account of when the Lord comes "to execute judgment upon all, and to convince all that are ungodly among them of all their ungodly deeds which they have ungodly committed, and of all their hard speeches which ungodly sinners have spoken against him" (Jude 15).

Paul, writing to the Thessalonians, says that "the Lord Jesus shall be revealed, . . . in flaming fire taking vengeance on them that know not God, and that obey not the gospel of our Lord Jesus Christ: who shall be punished with everlasting destruction from the presence of the Lord, and from the glory of his power" (II Thess. 1:7-9).

The doctrine of the second coming of Christ is not popular. It is a sad prospect for any but those who are truly born again. Men like to talk about the gentle Galilean and the pattern of His noble life here on earth, but not of the Great Judge returning in power to pour out divine wrath and vengeance on this sinful world. Christ will come to restore all the blessings that were lost in the fall and to usher in the millennium, but judgment must precede blessing, and there can be no universal righteousness until Satan and his ungodly followers are vanquished completely.

THE REIGN OF CHRIST

The Throne of Christ

The Throne of David (II Sam. 7:10-17; Ps. 89:3; Isa. 9:6; Jer. 23:5; Amos 9:11; Luke 1:32, 33; John 18:37; 19:19-22)

Nothing is plainer in all Scripture than the message of the angel to Mary, that her child "shall be called the Son of the Highest: and the Lord God shall give unto him the throne of his father David." One thousand years before, God had covenanted with David that He would establish his kingdom *forever* through a ruler that should come from his own family. This covenant was confirmed by the prophets. Amos goes so far as to speak of the restoration of the house of David, which in his day was already tottering. When Nebuchadnezzar carried away into captivity the royal family of Judah, he little realized that in that remnant, in due time, there was to be born a king far greater than himself.

No man of the house of David had better throne rights than Jesus Christ. In Matthew 1:1-16 we have the royal line from David to Joseph. The man who had throne rights when Christ was born was Joseph, the carpenter. However, it was not to Joseph, but to Mary, that the coming of the King was announced. Joseph was not the father of the divine King, and therefore no claim to the throne could be made through him. But Luke 3:23-31 gives us the genealogy of Joseph's father-in-law, or Mary's father. He too was a direct descendant of David through Nathan, a brother of Solomon. It is through this connection that Jesus Christ could lay valid claim to the throne of David. And we find that was just what He was expected to do.

When Jesus was finally born, Wise Men came from the East saying, "Where is he that is born King of the Jews?" Herod was so alarmed lest the royal child should dethrone him, that he slaughtered all the innocent babes of Bethlehem (Matt. 2:1-8, 16).

A little later, we find John the Baptist announcing that "the kingdom of heaven is at hand." The King Himself used the same expression at the beginning of His public ministry, and later directed His disciples to proclaim that message. Eight times the King was acclaimed "the son of David," and during His last week His royal rights were notably recognized. He admitted to Pilate that He had been born to sit on a throne — the throne of His father David — and the Roman governor wrote that title in three languages, and thus proclaimed to the world that Christ was the King. All the protests of the Jews that this significant statement be modified were in vain. Christ was King even in death.

The Throne at Jerusalem (Isa. 24:23; Jer. 3:17; Joel 3:16; Amos 1:2; Mic. 4:7)

From some of the songs that are sung, or sermons that are preached today, one would receive the impression that Zion is simply a synonym for heaven. However, in most Bible references Zion is identical with Jerusalem. From the time the stronghold of Zion was captured by David (II Sam. 5:7) and hallowed by placing the ark of the covenant upon it, there has been an interchange of the names of this mountain and the city of which it is a part (Ps. 135:21; Isa. 30:19; Zech. 1:14).

The throne of David which the angel promised the Son of Mary was to be in Jerusalem. So the prophets had stated, and so the people believed. After our Lord had performed the marvelous miracle of feeding the five thousand, the multitude was so firmly convinced that He was the promised Messiah that they endeavored to take Him by force to make Him King (John 6:14, 15).

THE KINGDOM OF CHRIST

A Universal Kingdom (Ps. 72:8-11; Dan. 2:44; 7:14; Zech. 14:9; Rev. 11:15)

This kingdom will not be limited to the confines of Solomon's domain, nor will the King reign merely over Israel. "He shall have dominion also from sea to sea . . . The kings of Tarshish and of the isles shall bring presents: the kings of Sheba and Seba shall offer gifts . . . All kings shall fall down before him: all nations shall serve him."

Babylon, Persia, Greece, and Rome established world kingdoms but, although twenty centuries have elapsed, no nation has been able to control the world. Mohammed attempted it, and so did Napoleon, but all the efforts of world conquerors have failed. The unbroken word of prophecy long ago predicted that the God of heaven will set up a kingdom that will never be destroyed or inherited by others, but will consume all other kingdoms. It is only when the kingdoms of this world become the kingdoms of our Lord Jesus Christ, that this prophecy will be fulfilled.

A Millennial Kingdom (Isa. 65:20, 22, 23; Rev. 20:4-6)

Six times in Revelation 20 we are told that the Lord will reign a thousand years. Because this coming age will last a thousand years, it has been called by the Latin word "millennium." While this specific number is not found elsewhere in Scripture, there are a multitude of promises for Israel, the nations of the earth, and even for all creation, which will require a millennium of years to be fulfilled.

Before the flood, men lived to be nearly a thousand years old. Sin in their lives, as well as the curse of sin on the earth, gradually reduced their longevity to but a fraction of what the patriarchs enjoyed. Discouraged and delayed in their projects, and worn and weakened in body, men today cannot live even a tenth of a millenium.

But when the curse of creation is removed and the long reign of righteousness begins, a person dying at the age of one hundred years will be considered a mere child. In other words, those dying at one hundred, which is one-tenth of a millennium — a thousand years being the ordinary time of life for those days — will be as proportionately young as a child of seven is today, since he has already lived one-tenth of the years allotted to man in this dispensation (Ps. 90:10). Longer life will not only permit men to enjoy that for which they have labored but, the accumulated knowledge and experience of centuries from which men can benefit, will be of untold value in improving their living conditions.

A Peaceful Kingdom

The Prince of Peace will be on the throne and consequently there will be:

Destruction of All Armaments (Isa. 2:4; Mic. 4:3)

There cannot be a warless world as long as nations continue to build armaments for the destruction of the human race. The Prince of Peace "shall rebuke strong nations afar off," and of their own accord they "shall beat their swords into plowshares, and their spears into pruning hooks." The books and newspapers of that day will not be filled with accounts of warring nations, and it will be literally true that they shall learn war no more.

Universal Knowledge of God (Jer. 31:34; Hab. 2:14)

During the Kingdom Age Christ will be recognized in all His perfection and knowledge; consequently there will be a general knowledge of God. "After those days, saith the Lord, I will put my law in their inward parts, and write it in their hearts; and will be their God, and they shall be my people . . . and they shall all know me, from the least of them unto the greatest of them" (Jer. 31:34). The Apostle Paul in the New Testament also speaks of this coming day when "at the name of Jesus every knee shall bow, of things in heaven, and things in earth, and things under the earth; And that every tongue shall confess that Jesus Christ is Lord, to the glory of God the Father" (Phil. 2:10, 11).

Individual Security (I Kings 4:25; Mic. 4:4)

The families of Judah and Israel enjoyed the most prosperous tranquility all the days of Solomon, whose reign is a type of that of the glory age. Under the wise administration of an impartial Judge, there will be an equitable division of the land and every man will be a proprietor. Not only will he have a possession of his own, but his life and property will be secure. The vine and the fig tree are mentioned rather than a house, to signify that there will be no need for a shelter. Men will be safe even in the fields and open air.

A Righteous Kingdom (Ps. 72:2-4, 12-14; Isa. 11:1-5; 61:11; Jer. 23:5)

In these days it is impossible for human governments and rulers to govern righteously. Our courts are unable to get at the facts even when all concerned are honestly trying to do so. Often lying witnesses and fraudulent lawyers and even untrustworthy judges conspire to thwart the course of justice. Might often makes right and wealth covers wickedness. But the King of the millennial kingdom will have all wisdom to know and all power to accomplish. He and His associate judges will not need to hear evidence or depend on witnesses, nor will it be necessary to employ armies or police forces to execute justice (Isa. 11:3, 4). Judgment will be meted out without delay on everyone who violates the laws. "He shall deliver the needy when he crieth; the poor also and him that hath no helper."

Can we who seek first the kingdom of God and His righteousness, and pray, "Thy kingdom come," possibly picture the joy of a thousand years of peace? The government of an absolute monarch too wise to make any mistakes and too good to be unkind, yet powerful enough to secure the absolute submission of all, will be perfect.

REVIEW QUESTIONS

1. How many references to the second coming of the Lord Jesus Christ are in the New Testament?
2. What statement was made on the occasion of our Lord's ascension that would indicate His return in person?
3. What two passages in Scripture state that He will return with His saints?
4. What did the Gospel writers say about His return in power and glory?
5. How do we know that the second coming will be for judgment upon unbelievers?
6. What is meant by the throne of David and where is it to be established?
7. How are the throne rights of Christ revealed in the genealogies of Matthew and Luke?
8. How do we know that Christ's kingdom will be universal?
9. What passages in Scripture state the length of Christ's reign upon earth?
10. What three circumstances will make it possible for this to be a reign of peace?
11. From what Scriptures do we know that there will be universal knowledge of God?
12. What assurance is given that Christ's reign will be a righteous reign?

APPLYING DOCTRINE TO LIFE

1. How can a teacher "watch" for Christ's return while busy in a teaching ministry?
2. What are you doing for the Lord now which will not be necessary after His second coming?

THE PERSONALITY AND POWER OF THE HOLY SPIRIT

11

There are some things which we cannot see but which we most certainly believe. In fact, four of our five senses may be closed to the reality of certain facts which our fifth sense proclaims.

No one has seen a pain, heard it, or smelled it, but one can *feel* a pain. The wind cannot be seen, but we know that it bends the trees and tosses the waves. Electricity cannot be seen, but we know that it exists, as is evident by its power all about us.

THE PERSONALITY OF THE HOLY SPIRIT

No man has ever seen the Holy Spirit. But the evidences of His presence and power are conclusive to all who are willing to give unbiased thought to the phenomena which His presence brings to pass.

We have learned that the three persons of the Godhead are equal in power and glory. Many of their common attributes we have already studied, so that now we need to study only those attributes of the Holy Spirit which relate especially to the believer in Christ. Because there are those who would not only deny the deity but also the *personality of the Holy Spirit,* it is essential to begin our study at this point.

The lessons on God's works of creation and providence helped us understand the personality of God. The incarnation, miracles, and resurrection are conclusive evidence of the personality of Jesus Christ. But the acts and workings of the Holy Spirit are so secret and mystical — so much is said about His influence, gifts, and power — that some have hastily concluded that He is a manifestation or influence of the divine nature rather than a person. His being called "breath," "wind," "power," and His association with symbols as "oil," "fire," and "water," have erroneously led some to think of Him as an impersonal influence emanating from God.

Is it essential to know whether or not the Holy Spirit is a person? If the Holy Spirit is a person, He is worthy of our worship, faith, and love; and the Christian has no right to withhold honor due Him. If the Holy Spirit is a person, infinitely wise, holy, and loving, then it should be our concern that He possess us and use us to His honor and glory. It makes all the difference in the world whether we vainly struggle to possess the Holy Spirit or whether the Holy Spirit possesses us.

Trinity of Persons

How many times we have sung the "Doxology" without thinking of the words! Surely we should not sing this tribute of adoration to the Trinity without realizing that we have ascribed to the Holy Spirit the same devout praise which is accorded to the Father and to the Son. "Glory be to the Father, and to the Son, and to the Holy Ghost." The singing of the "Gloria" is the proclamation both of the deity and the personality of the Holy Spirit. If we grant personality to the Father and to the Son, of necessity the third person of the Godhead must be included. The Bible provides proof in:

Creation (Gen. 1:26)

When God created man He said, "Let *us* make man," not, "Let *me*." The three members of the Godhead said, "Let us unitedly become the Creator of man." In the plan of redemption it was the same three persons speaking with one consent. "Let *us* save man." It is a source of sweet comfort to think that it was not one person, but the glorious Trinity who declared unitedly, "*We* will save man."

Baptism (Matt. 28:19)

Baptism is administered in the name of the Father, and of the Son, and of the Holy Ghost. No one thinks of the Holy Spirit as a power or a force in this connection. He is a person.

Benediction (II Cor. 13:14)

How familiar is the benediction taken from the Scriptures with which our services are concluded! Here again the Holy Spirit is ascribed an equal place with that of the Father and the Son. "The grace of the Lord Jesus Christ, and the love of God, and the communion of the Holy Spirit be with you all."

Divine Attributes

Not only is personality ascribed to the Holy Spirit through His association with the other members of the Godhead, but the attributes of the divine nature are also recorded of Him.

He Is Eternal (Heb. 9:14)

It is important to note that though the believer possesses eternal life, he had a beginning in time. Actually, all men, though creatures of time, will exist forever either in bliss or in judgment. However, God has neither beginning nor end, but eternally exists.

He Is Omnipresent (Ps. 139:7-10)

The Holy Spirit is everywhere present, "Whither shall I go from thy spirit? or whither shall I flee from thy presence?"

He Is Omnipotent

The virgin birth of our Lord (Luke 1:35) was made possible by the omnipotence of the Holy Spirit, who has no limitations in power.

We marvel at the unpromising group of men our Lord chose to carry on His work after His departure. They were men without learning, money, or influence. Moreover, despite His revelation of

Himself to them, they were so lacking in faith and courage as to desert Him at the hour of His arrest and trial. Yet these men later created such a stir, not only in Jerusalem but throughout Asia and Europe, that people said, "These that have turned the world upside down are come hither also." It was not these men who transformed the world but the omnipotent power of the Holy Spirit working through them (Acts 4:31-33; 17:6).

He Is Omniscient

Paul, a great scholar, intellectually well-equipped to deal with the keen-minded Greeks, humbly acknowledged to them that his preaching "was not with enticing words of man's wisdom, but in demonstration of the Spirit and of power" (I Cor. 2:1-11).

Personal Characteristics

Personal Address

The Greek word for "spirit" is neuter and should be accompanied by a neuter pronoun. However, contrary to ordinary usage, the masculine pronoun is used 12 times in John 16:7, 8, 13, 14. This is not just personification, but a definite assertion of the personality of the Holy Spirit. This does not mean that the third person of the Trinity has hands and feet like a man. We must distinguish between personality and corporeality. A *person* can think, feel, and exercise will power. All these functions are attributed to the Holy Spirit in Scripture.

Personal Attributes

Intellect

The Holy Spirit has a mind (Rom. 8:27) — the unique possession of a person. He searches the deepest truths of God, and possesses enough knowledge of His counsels to understand His purposes (I Cor. 2:10, 11). Could a mere influence do this?

Emotion (Rom. 15:30)

Have you ever thought of "the *love* of the Holy Spirit"? The love of the Father was infinitely great. His love was broad enough to encompass the entire world, and great enough to give His only begotten, beloved Son for its salvation. The love of the Son was also inconceivably great. His love caused Him to leave the glory of heaven, and come and die for sinful men. Yet the great love of the Father would have been in vain, and the self-sacrificing love of the Son to no purpose, if it had not been for the great, patient, infinite love of the blessed Spirit working in our hearts. The love of Father, Son, and Holy Spirit is expressed in the divine program for the salvation of the sinner.

Will

The Holy Spirit has a will of His own (I Cor. 12:11; Acts 16:6, 7). It is quite different with the angels, that do God's commandments, hearkening unto the voice of *His word* (Ps. 103:20).

Paul desired to preach in the province of Asia, but the Holy Spirit willed otherwise. Later he was privileged to minister for two years in Ephesus, a key city there (Acts 19:10).

Human Attitudes

Grieved

We could not grieve the Holy Spirit if He were merely a force or an influence. Alas, we can hurt His feelings. Every unkind word, every selfish deed, every impure thought grieves the Spirit (Eph. 4:30).

Resisted

Stephen delivered one of the most masterful sermons in the Bible and so antagonized the Jews that they stoned him to death. In his dying message he declared that, generation after generation, Israel had persisted in *resisting* the Holy Spirit (Acts 7:51).

THE POWER OF THE HOLY SPIRIT

In the Gospels the disciples are cowards; in the book of Acts they are heroes. A mere maid frightened Peter, but a few days later that same man was as bold as a lion. Courageously he stood before a multitude of three thousand and charged them with the crucifixion of the Lord Jesus Christ. What made the difference? The power of the Holy Spirit. In His parting message to the disciples just before His ascension, Christ said, "Ye shall receive power after that the Holy Ghost is come upon you" (Acts 1:8). So conspicuous was this power in the life of Peter, that Simon the magician offered him money saying, "Give me also this power." To this Peter replied, "Thy money perish with thee, because thou hast thought that the gift of God may be purchased with money" (Acts 8:18-20).

In Creation (Gen. 1:2, 3; 2:7; Job 26:13; Ps. 104:30)

The Holy Spirit shared in the creation of the heaven and the earth. In other lessons we have noticed that the work of creation was attributed to God the Father and Christ the Son. This is not contradictory, but is one more proof of the Trinity. "Let *us* make man" (Gen. 1:26).

All the stars of heaven are said to have been placed aloft by the Spirit, and one particular constellation called the "crooked serpent" is especially pointed out as His handiwork. We do not know how remote the time of creation nor through what various stages of existence our planets have passed, but we do read that at the beginning of creation "the earth was without form and void, and darkness was upon the face of the deep" (Gen. 1:2). It was then that "the Spirit of God moved upon the face of the waters" (Gen. 1:2), bringing order out of chaos and causing darkness to disappear. All this happened before the creation of man. It was the Spirit of God who breathed into man the very life of his existence, and it is the same

Spirit who perpetuates life and "renewest the face of the earth" by the creation of all life.

In Regeneration (John 3:3-5; Eph. 3:16; Titus 3:5)

Nicodemus was a rich man and was held in high esteem among the people. He had education and honor, for he was one of the seventy who sat in the highest council of the Jews. But he lacked one thing — life from God. Christ told him that he must be born again. In his natural birth he was born to die. Why? Because by one man, Adam, "sin entered into the world, and death by sin; and so death passed upon all men, for that all have sinned" (Rom. 5:12).

Regeneration, then, is re-creation. If creation is the work of the Holy Spirit, it is not surprising that the work of re-creation is also ascribed to Him. Men cannot create themselves or re-create themselves. Men cannot create a tiny gnat or a grain of sand; nor can we find a thing which has created itself. Nothing but the power of the Holy Spirit is equal to this task.

We must distinguish between Christ's work *for* us and the Holy Spirit's work *in us*. Without the sacrifice upon Golgotha, it would have been impossible for man to be saved. Without the work of the Holy Spirit it would be equally impossible. The Holy Spirit creates in our hearts the faith through which we recognize and receive salvation.

Regeneration is never separated from faith. The moment a man really believes on Christ, however feebly, he is regenerated by the Holy Spirit. The weakness of his faith may make him unconscious of the change, just as a newborn infant knows little or nothing about himself. But where there is faith there is always a new birth, and where there is not faith there is no regeneration.

In Inspiration

Since the Holy Spirit is the author of the Scriptures, it is not surprising to find a peculiar power emanating from the Bible which is not found in any other book (Jer. 5:14; 23:29; II Cor. 3:6; I Thess. 1:5; Heb. 4:12).

A poor man in South Africa once met Mr. Moffat, the missionary, with a distressed look. Mr. Moffat asked him what was the matter, and he replied, "My dog has swallowed three leaves of the New Testament."

"Why cry over that?"

"Because it will spoil the dog. He was a good hunter, but it will make him tame now, the same as it makes all the people tame around here. It will spoil him as a hunter."

The man had seen the wonderful effect of the reading and preaching of the Bible — that it made people quiet and contented — and he was afraid it would have the same effect upon his dog.

Thousands of men have been converted simply from reading the

Word of God. It was that which first awakened Martin Luther to the emptiness of the popish doctrine of works, and gave him courage to nail his ninety-five propositions upon the door of the Wittenburg Cathedral in defiance of the powerful Church of Rome.

In Witnessing

When the Holy Spirit descended upon our Lord at His baptism, it was to attest or witness to the fact that He was the Son of God. Afterward, when the Lord stilled the storm, healed the sick, raised the dead, and cast out demons, it was done by the power of the Holy Spirit (Isa. 61:1; Zech. 4:6; Luke 4:16-21). These were works of attestation, works which authenticated or bore witness to His power.

When Christ in His farewell address declared that His disciples would perform even greater works than He had done (John 14:12), it was because the same Holy Spirit who empowered Him, would rest upon them. Just before He left them, He announced that they would receive power after that the Holy Ghost was come upon them, and they would be witnesses for Him (Acts 1:8). Ten days later, the Holy Spirit came like a mighty rushing wind, and His great power was soon evident, not only in Jerusalem, but in Judea and Samaria and the regions beyond. "With great power gave the apostles witness of the resurrection of the Lord Jesus" (Acts 4:33). But the disciples fully realized the secret of their power and were not ashamed to disclose it. "We are his witnesses of these things; and so is also the Holy Ghost, whom God hath given to them that obey him" (Acts 5:32). The Holy Spirit, as our Lord predicted, convicted that great multitude at Pentecost "of sin, and of righteousness, and of judgment."

The Holy Spirit attested to the message and ministry of the disciples by many miraculous deeds (Heb. 2:4). Not only were the disciples given the ability to speak in the languages of eighteen different nationalities represented at Pentecost, but miracles of life and healing followed. Peter healed Aeneas and raised Dorcas from the dead. So numerous were the healings of the sick that invalids lined the streets where Peter walked, that the efficacy of his shadow falling on them might afford recovery (Acts 5:12-16). Prison doors were thrown open and prisoners released to the astonishment of the authorities who had taken every precaution to prevent an escape. Again and again Paul and his companions were miraculously saved from stoning, from prison, from shipwreck (Rom. 15:18, 19). These are the acts, not of the apostles, but of the Holy Spirit who was the might and marvel of the early Church.

In the Resurrection

The resurrection of Christ is ascribed to the work of the Holy Spirit. We may well be perplexed to find that sometimes the resurrection of Christ is ascribed to Himself; that because of His own power He could not be held by the bond of death. He willingly laid down His life and He had the power to take it up again (John 10:17). But in another portion of Scripture our Lord's resurrection is ascribed to God the Father: "Whom God hath raised from the dead" (Acts 3:15); "Him hath God exalted" (Acts 5:31). Scripture also teaches that Christ was raised by the Holy Spirit (Rom. 1:4; 8:11; I Pet. 3:18). This difference in the divine record instead of contradicting the truth merely confirms it. The difficulty is easily explained by the doctrine of the Holy Trinity, which declares that the three persons in the Godhead are the same in substance and equal in power and glory.

REVIEW QUESTIONS

1. How do we know that the Holy Spirit is a person?
2. What three Scripture passages include the Holy Spirit in the Trinity?
3. Name four divine attributes of the Holy Spirit.
4. Suggest three personal attributes.
5. What do we mean by the human attitudes of the Holy Spirit?
6. In what five ways is the power of the Holy Spirit manifested?
7. How is the power of the Holy Spirit manifested in regeneration?
8. In what respect is the Holy Spirit the author of Scripture?
9. How did the miracles of our Lord relate to the power of the Holy Spirit?
10. How do we know that the Holy Spirit participated in the work of creation?
11. What did Christ mean when He declared to His disciples that they would perform even greater works than He had done?
12. Give scriptural evidence of proof that the resurrection of Christ is ascribed to the work of the Holy Spirit.

APPLYING DOCTRINE TO LIFE

1. How is the personality and power of the Holy Spirit manifested in the life of a teacher?
2. How should the Spirit's authorship of the Scriptures affect a teacher's presentation of them?

THE HOLY SPIRIT AND THE BELIEVER

12

Christ was about to return to heaven. It was the last hour with His disciples. He was about to leave His earthly office as Teacher and Prophet. But before doing so, He wished to acquaint them with the one who would come after Him. He prepared their hearts and aroused their interest in the one who was to follow by saying, "It is expedient for you that I go away; for if I go not away, the Comforter will not come unto you; but if I depart, I will send him unto you" (John 16:7). "I will pray the Father, and he shall give you another Comforter, that he may abide with you forever" (John 14:16).

The word "Comforter," while most fitting for the needs of the grief-stricken disciples, does not fully describe the service that the Holy Spirit would render. The name *Paraclete* in the Greek has no translation that exactly reproduces its meaning. The same word elsewhere indicates the office of Christ in Heaven: "We have an *advocate* with the Father" (I John 2:1). But the Holy Spirit was to be even more than a trustworthy attorney for the disciples. He was to be their Teacher, Partner, Companion — in fact, everything that Christ had been to them.

THE BELIEVER TAUGHT BY THE HOLY SPIRIT

Jesus Christ had been the official teacher of the Twelve. They did not sit at the feet of the scribes and Pharisees to learn their doctrines, but listened with rapt attention to Him who "spake as never man spake." "And now," said He, "when I am gone, where will you find the great infallible teacher? Shall I set you up a pope at Rome to whom you shall go? Shall I ordain the councils of the Church to solve your problems?" Christ said no such thing. "I am the infallible Teacher, and when I am gone I will send you another Teacher who shall be the authoritative oracle of God. He will guide you into all truth." The promise was made in the first instance to the apostles, but later it was applied to all believers. Each believer may be independent of human teachers — "ye need not that any man teach you." It is the privilege of each of us to be "taught of God." The man who is most fully taught of God is the very one who will be most ready to listen to what God has taught others. Why is the Holy Spirit the preeminent, infallible Teacher?

He is the Author of the Scriptures (John 16:13; II Tim. 3:16; II Pet. 1:20, 21; Rev. 2:7)

Peter tells us that the men who wrote the Scriptures were moved

— "borne along" — by the Holy Spirit. Paul declares that all Scripture is "given by inspiration of God," or more literally, is "God-breathed." As God breathed into man the breath of life and made him a living soul, so the Holy Spirit breathed into human beings a living knowledge of the things of God. It was "what the Spirit saith unto the churches" that John was commanded to hear and record; and it was the Spirit who was to guide the apostles into all truth, and show them things to come.

He is the Interpreter of Scripture (John 16:13, 14; I Cor. 2:10)

As the author of all Scripture, surely the divine Spirit should be capable of understanding it and explaining it. The best commentary on the Bible is the Bible itself. By comparing Scripture with Scripture we may have an infallible interpretation of all divine utterances.

He Was the Companion of Christ

Not only was Christ born of the Spirit (Luke 1:35), and raised from the dead in the power of the Spirit (Rom. 1:4; 8:11), but He was:

Anointed by the Spirit (Acts 10:38)

Before He entered upon His active ministry, our Savior was anointed by the Holy Spirit for service.

Led by the Spirit (Matt. 4:1)

After His baptism, the Holy Spirit, who had descended upon Christ in the form of a dove, led Him into the wilderness to be tempted by Satan.

He Instructs the Believer

About Christ (John 15:26; 16:13-15)

The Holy Spirit reveals and glorifies Christ as cannot be done by any other. The disciples knew Christ, but they knew Him as a man. The Holy Spirit reveals Him in a much greater and grander manner. You have known a man by his appearance, by his face. Now you come to know him by his character. He reveals himself by his abilities, by his integrity, by his truthfulness, as your friend.

About Spiritual Things (I Cor. 2:9-14)

We have already observed that the Holy Spirit is the author and the interpreter of the Word of God. The inward illumination of the Holy Spirit enables us to understand the Word. It is a great mistake to try to comprehend spiritual revelation with natural understanding. A man with no aesthetic sense might as well expect to appreciate the Sistine Madonna because he is not color-blind, as an unspiritual man to understand the Bible simply because he understands the language in which the Bible was written. All the wisdom of Greece could not enable the Corinthians to understand spiritual things, and all the intellects of our greatest universities will be mystified by spiritual truth without the instruction of the Holy Spirit.

He Reproves the World (John 16:7-11)

The world cannot receive or know the Holy Spirit, as He dwells only with the believer. The Holy Spirit, however, works through the believer to reprove the world:

Of Sin (John 16:9)

Not of all *sins,* such as intemperance, greed, theft, falsehood, but of *one special sin* — the sin of rejecting Jesus Christ as the Savior of the world. Sin received new meaning when Christ came into the world (John 15:22). Christlessness in a Christian land is atheism. The Holy Spirit makes a man see that not to believe in Christ is the crowning sin, since it makes God a liar. He who believes not on Christ has rejected God's mercy and despised the grandest display of God's love.

Of Righteousness

Christ was the only man who was truly righteous. The scribes and Pharisees emphasized keeping the law and thought they were almost perfect; but our Lord said, "Except your righteousness shall exceed the righteousness of the scribes and Pharisees ye shall in no case enter into the kingdom of heaven." Now the only righteous one was about to leave the world, but the Holy Spirit was to come and convince the world of the righteousness of the Lord Jesus Christ and the unrighteousness of all others (John 16:10).

Of Judgment

The death of Christ caused judgment to be passed upon Satan, and he realized that his kingdom was virtually overthrown. Our Lord recognized Satan as the prince of this world and He saw him lurking behind Judas, Peter, and the Pharisees. It was Satan's "works" that Christ came to destroy, and his "death-fearing" subjects that He came to deliver. Calvary was the decisive battlefield. Satan was judged and condemned. He now awaits sentence, which shall be executed when the kingdoms of this world become the kingdoms of our Lord Jesus Christ. The Holy Spirit will convince the world that "the prince of this world" is doomed and all his subjects with him (John 16:11).

THE BELIEVER GUIDED BY THE HOLY SPIRIT

As Jesus Christ is now the believer's advocate before God, so the Holy Spirit is God's advocate before men. Have you ever seen an earnest minister pleading with hands uplifted and eyes filled with tears? Were his skill and power acquired in college or seminary? Ah, no. It was the Holy Spirit within him advocating His cause aright.

Guidance in Worship

The only true and acceptable worship is that which the Holy

Spirit prompts and directs (John 4:23; Phil. 3:3). A man may be earnest in his worship, and still not have submitted himself to the guidance of the Holy Spirit. In utter self-distrust and self-abnegation we must cast ourselves upon the Holy Spirit to lead us aright in our:

Prayers

The disciples did not know how to pray as they ought, and said to Jesus, "Lord, teach us to pray" (Luke 11:1). We do not know how to pray as we ought, but we have another Paraclete right at hand to help (Rom. 8:26, 27; Eph. 6:18; Jude 20). When we cast ourselves completely upon our advocate, He directs our prayers, leads our desires, and guides our utterances. "The prayer that God the Holy Spirit inspires is the prayer that God the Father answers."

Praise

A prominent characteristic of the Spirit-filled life is thanksgiving (Eph. 5:18-20). This, like prayer, to be acceptable to God, must be directed by the Holy Spirit. One reason why the singing of psalms, done sincerely, is worship acceptable to God, is because the Holy Spirit is the author of these immortal hymns of praise.

Guidance in the Affairs of Life

The Holy Spirit selects our field of activity and directs us to it (Acts 8:26-29; 13:2, 4; 16:6, 7). He opens the door to the place where He would have us labor, and closes the door to the task which we might ourselves select. He also directs us to the individual to whom God desires that we should speak. There is so much to do for Christ and so many to whom we might speak in His behalf. Physical limitations, however, curtail our efforts. How are we to know what to do and what not to do? The Holy Spirit will guide us. There are certain places we are to go and certain people to whom we are to speak. If we walk in obedience to the Word, the Holy Spirit will arrange our contacts with the very persons we can best reach with the gospel, and not only so, but He will make those contacts at just the right time.

Guidance in Time of Trial

The disciples were not to worry about securing an able lawyer when they were on trial for life. The Holy Spirit would be their advocate when they were brought before governors and kings. How was it that Stephen could plead so ably before the blindly prejudiced council which was determined to execute him? The answer is that they were not able to resist the wisdom and the Spirit by which he spoke. The Jews hired a noted Roman lawyer named Tertullus to prosecute their case against Paul, but to no avail (Acts 24:1, 22). And how was it that this prisoner in chains could plead so powerfully before the Roman governor that Felix trembled before him, and rose up hurriedly to dismiss the case? (Acts 24:25).

It was not the man who pleaded, but God the Holy Spirit who was pleading through him.

THE BELIEVER CONTROLLED BY THE HOLY SPIRIT

We are told that no one can call Jesus Lord except by the Holy Ghost (I Cor. 12:3). It is this work of leading the believer to realize the Lordship of Jesus in his life, that the Spirit desires to accomplish in the life of every child of God. For it is a sad fact that while many have accepted Christ as Savior, He is not complete master of their lives. Many are delivered from the guilt of sin and from its ultimate penalty, but all do not know the blessedness of His Lordship. We receive Him as Savior by faith on the ground of His finished work on Calvary; but He did that *for* us only that He might do something *in* us.

A Spirit-Possessed Life — Holiness

Things were going wrong in the Corinthian church. A spirit of contention was dividing its members. The people were converted to Peter, Paul, and Apollos, and not to Christ (I Cor. 1:12). Grave sin and immorality were prevalent. The members for the most part were interested in worldly things. What was the cause? The Holy Spirit was not allowed to exercise His power.

Paul did not tell these Corinthian Christians that they were without the Holy Spirit who had led them in the public confession of their faith to declare that Jesus was the Son of God (I Cor. 12:3). They could not have been Christians without the Holy Spirit (Rom. 8:9). It was their failure to recognize the presence of the Holy Spirit dwelling within them (I Cor. 3:16; 6:19) and their failure to permit Him to control their lives, for which the apostle took them to task. In the foul atmosphere of that heathen city the Christians were exposed to fearful temptations, and needed a superhuman power if they were to keep themselves pure.

What honor, what dignity have been conferred upon these corruptible bodies that they should be chosen as the dwelling place of the Holy Spirit! The body of the Christian is claimed and taken possession of by the God who has redeemed it, and therefore it should be treated with the same respect with which the Jews regarded the Holy of Holies. The Christian who thus thinks of his flesh cannot fail to acquire a higher regard for it. How reverently he should guard his eyes to keep them from unlawful scenes! How zealously he should watch his tongue to keep it from evil words! How diligently he should preserve his thoughts and affections from evil, since God has claimed his members as His own and bidden him to give them wholly to Him!

A Spirit-Sealed Life — Assurance

The presence of the Holy Spirit not only gives the believer

power to live a holy life, well pleasing to God, when he recognizes what that life is, but He takes us, as it were, by the hand and leads us into that life (Rom. 8:14, 16; Eph. 1:13; 4:30). This is the most convincing of all evidence given the Christian to prove his heavenly heritage.

A martyr is going to the stake — thousands of Christian martyrs have perished in this way. The crowds are mocking, but on he goes with courageous tread. Now they bind him with a chain about his waist. They heap fagots all about him. The flame is lighted, but he is speaking: "Bless the Lord, O my soul." The flames are kindling around his legs, but he lifts his hands and cries, "I know that my Redeemer liveth, and though the fire devours this body, yet in my flesh shall I see God!" His body is being consumed, but he sings amid the torture, and finally cries triumphantly, "Into Thy hand I commit my spirit." What gives this man such assurance? (II Tim. 2:19-21). It is the glorious witness of the Holy Spirit that he is a son of God (Gal. 4:6).

A Spirit-Filled Life — Service

The phrase "full of the Holy Ghost" is a familiar one in the New Testament. Our Lord Himself performed His earthly ministry in the Holy Spirit's fullness and power. Again and again the record states that the disciples were filled with the Holy Spirit. At Pentecost the 120 disciples "were all filled with the Holy Ghost" (Acts 2:4). This was to prepare them for the service they were to render in the founding of the Church. Peter stood up and faced the great congregation which had been so outspoken in their hostility to Christ and His disciples, and the lives of three thousand were transformed in a day. A little later, when opposition had set in and the disciples were brought before the council, Peter, "filled with the Holy Ghost," made a masterly defense which resulted in their being liberated. In the prayer meeting which followed, "the place was shaken where they were assembled together; and they were all filled with the Holy Ghost" (Acts 4:31).

Paul, in his letter to the Ephesians (5:18), lays that obligation on every believer in Christ when he says, "And be not drunk with wine, wherein is excess; but be filled with the Spirit." Therefore it is the privilege and obligation of every believer in Christ not only to have the Holy Spirit dwelling within him, but to be filled with the Spirit.

The promise has been given — "He that believeth on me, as the scripture hath said, from within him shall flow rivers of living water. (But this spake he of the Spirit, which they that believe on him should receive)" (John 7:38, 39). Only service done in the power of the Holy Spirit counts for eternity. We see the Spirit of God pictured as the great life-giving river which seeks an outlet for the divine outflow of life and love in everyday practical ministry to others. It begins to flow as soon as it finds a channel. It keeps flowing so long as the channel remains open.

A Victorious Life — Fruitfulness (Rom. 5:5; 8:2, 9-13; 14:17; Gal. 5:17, 22, 23)

When a believer is regenerated and the Holy Spirit condescends to take up His abode in his body, he discovers that he has two natures — his bodily and his spiritual. He finds that his body is still subject to the temptations of the flesh. Such a struggle as goes on between the good and evil within is well depicted in the seventh chapter of Romans: "For I know that in me (that is, in my flesh), dwelleth no good thing: for to will is present with me; but how to perform that which is good I find not" (Rom. 7:18). The Holy Spirit has not been taken into consideration in the terrible conflict of the seventh chapter, but He is mentioned nineteen times in connection with the life of victory described in the eighth chapter. The rule of the Holy Spirit in the life of the believer is his secret of victory over sin.

The place and prominence that the believer gives to the Holy Spirit will determine his character. We are not born with a fixed nature. Character is the result of our habits, and these are repeated actions. The character of the natural man who lives to gratify his body is a sad and sickening spectacle. The awful catalog of the works of the flesh is set forth in sharp contrast to the fruit of the Spirit (Gal. 5:19-21). The character of the spiritual man who allows the Holy Spirit to guide his life is altogether different. He produces the blessed fruit of the Christian life. There are three beautiful clusters to this fruit.

Love, Joy, Peace (Gal. 5:22)

This is our Christian experience in relation to God. It is only through a walk in subjection to the Holy Spirit that the love of God is shed abroad in our hearts (Rom. 5:5), and we share the joy of the Holy Spirit (Acts 13:52), and "the peace of God, which passeth all understanding" (Phil. 4:7).

Longsuffering, Gentleness, Goodness (Gal. 5:22)

This is our Christian experience in relation to our fellowmen. The Holy Spirit enables us to bear and forebear. First we give ourselves to the Lord, and then to those about us. We practice kindness and courtesy to all.

Faithfulness, Meekness, Self-Control (Gal. 5:22, 23)

This is our Christian experience in relation to ourselves. As we walk in the Spirit, we will be faithful and humble in all our duties, and exercise control over all our thoughts and actions. "Sin shall not have dominion over you" (Rom. 6:14).

REVIEW QUESTIONS

1. In what respects was the Holy Spirit to take the place of Christ in the lives of the disciples?
2. About what does the Holy Spirit instruct the believer?
3. Of what three things does the Holy Spirit reprove the world?
4. How does the Holy Spirit guide the believer in worship?
5. In what respect is the Holy Spirit a guide in the affairs of life?
6. Give several illustrations of how the Holy Spirit guided the apostles in time of trial.
7. In what four ways does the Holy Spirit control the life of the believer?
8. Show how members of the church at Corinth had not as yet experienced the Spirit-possessed life?
9. What do we mean by Spirit-sealed life?
10. What is the evidence of a Spirit-filled life?
11. What are the characteristics of a victorious life?
12. Which of the nine characteristics speak of the Christian experience in relation to God? Which in relation to his fellowmen? Which in relation to himself?

APPLYING DOCTRINE TO LIFE

1. To what measure can believers' lives be Spirit-filled today?
2. List at least five changes that should take place in your life as the result of a deepened understanding of our Triune God.